METAPHYSICAL DIVINE WISDOM

on Balancing the Mind, Body, and Soul

A Practical Motivational Guide to Spirituality
Series

KEVIN HUNTER

WARRIOR
OF LIGHT
PRESS

Warrior of Light Press
www.kevin-hunter.com

First Edition: July 2019
Printed in the United States of America

All rights reserved. Copyright © 2019
ISBN-13: 978-1733196239

3. Mind and Body. 2. Spirituality. 1. Title

DEDICATION

For you on your soul's spiritual journey.

METAPHYSICAL DIVINE WISDOM
BOOK SERIES

On Psychic Spirit Team Heaven Communication
On Soul Consciousness and Purpose
On Increasing Prayer with Faith for an Abundant Life
On Balancing the Mind, Body, and Soul
On Manifesting Fearless Assertive Confidence
On Universal, Physical, Spiritual and Soul Love

♥

Contents

Chapter 1 1
Raise Your Soul's Energy Vibration

Chapter 2 19
Fire Up Your Inner Child

Chapter 3 32
Nature's Therapy

Chapter 4 37
Elevating Your Mind, Body, and Spirit

Chapter 5 50
Expand Your Consciousness

Chapter 6 63
Detoxify Your Soul

Chapter 7 77
Soul Cleansing to Motivation

Chapter 8 89
Clearing the Chaos Within and Around Your World

Chapter 9 _____ 100
Gossip Machine to Centered Light

Chapter 10 _____ 115
Balancing Your Inner Spirit

Chapter 11 _____ 131
Rise Above the Mundane and Into the Divine

Chapter 12 _____ 146
Cord Cutting, Shielding, Grounding

Chapter 13 _____ 166
Vibrational Uplift

Chapter 14 _____ 181
The Balance of Masculine and Feminine Energies

Chapter 15 _____ 195
Twin Souls Yin and Yang

Chapter 16 _____ 204
Blissful Happy Place

AUTHOR NOTE

The *Metaphysical Divine Wisdom* books are a series of spiritually based books that focus on different areas of one's life. Like many of my spiritual related metaphysical books, this one is also infused with practical messages and spirit guidance that my Spirit team has taught and shared with me revolving around many different topics. The main goal is to fine-tune your body, mind, and soul. Like all souls, you are a Divine communicator capable of receiving messages and guidance from Heaven.

My personal Spirit team council makes up God and the Holy Spirit, as well as a team of guides, angels, and sometimes Archangels and Saints. I am merely the liaison or messenger in delivering and interpreting the intentions of what they wish to communicate. My team comprises some hard truth telling Wise Ones from the Other Side, including Saint Nathaniel, who can be brutal in his direct forcefulness. He cuts right to the heart of humanity without apology. I have learned quite a bit from him while adopting his ideology, which is Heaven's philosophy as a whole. I wouldn't preach Divine Guidance that God doesn't whisper into my Clairaudient ear first.

If I use the word "He" when pertaining to God, this does not mean that I am advocating that he is a male. Simply replace the word, "He" with one you are comfortable using to identify God for you to be. If the word, "God" makes you uncomfortable, then substitute it with one you're more familiar with like Universe, Spirit, Energy, the Light, or any other comparable word. This goes for any gender I use as examples. When I say, "spirit team", I am referring to a team of 'Guides and Angels'.

One of the purposes of my work is to empower, enlighten, as well as entertain. It's also to help you improve yourself, your soul, your life and humanity by default. If anything, I am preaching to myself, because God knows that I can use a refresher course once in a while. It does not matter if you are a beginner or well versed in the subject matter. There may be something that reminds you of something you already know or something that you were unaware of. We all have much to share with one another, as we are all one in the end.

~ Kevin Hunter

METAPHYSICAL DIVINE WISDOM
ON BALANCING THE MIND, BODY, AND SOUL

CHAPTER ONE

*Raise Your Soul's
Energy Vibration*

The mind, body, and soul is a genre that is widely accepted and known amongst all of the spiritual communities around the world. These key areas are the core parts of you to focus on improving if one were seeking to bring out your soul's profound state of happiness that exists in Heaven. The mind was put first because it is in the mind where all things become possible. When you expand your mind and consciousness, then the opportunities you can create out of this are infinite. When your mind deteriorates or functions on a lesser frequency, then being able to feed all other parts of you become limited, which has an overall effect on your health and wellness state to other important areas of your physical life. It is the mind that houses the dark part of your ego that runs rampant holding a loaded gun that aims and fires wherever it can. It is in your mind where you train yourself to either see positivity in your life or the negative. No one has any trouble being negative, but being positive takes enormous effort. When you alter your state of mind by the will of your thoughts, then there is no telling what you can accomplish when you set your mind to it.

Your soul's vibration is the overall energy that it vibrates at. When you have it set in your mind to take care of your physical body, then this is simultaneously taking care of your soul. Taking care of your physical body includes taking care of your mental and emotional state. You might be exceptionally physically fit, but if you're a toxic person, then you may as well be drinking as much alcohol as you can until you black out. It's that mental toxic state which creates the most damage to your soul. Being a toxic person is equitable to the high amounts of toxins that someone puts into their body.

One of the benefits to raising your vibration are that it assists you in picking up on Divinely guided psychic messages more easily. When you are able to efficiently pick up on those messages, then this equates to making solid choices in life that bring you closer to the threshold of abundance attainment. Improving all aspects of the mind, body, and soul are all connected to achieving greater heights in life both physically and spiritually.

When it comes to psychic phenomena, one of the bigger enticements that many want is to communicate more efficiently with the Other Side. The top reasons noticed is to see what their future holds. When will I meet my love partner? Is this person my soul mate? When will I find another job? When will I buy my first house? These are all physical material life desires, but this is not the main reason to improving one's psychic abilities. When someone's life hasn't been where it wants to be, then it worries about the future wondering if anything good will ever happen for them. This prompts them to pull cards or go to a psychic reader for help. The answers to your future lie within the core part of your soul because it's in your soul contract that you have access to when you raise your vibration and tune in to what is beyond.

This is a world filled with beings that wrestle with that dreadful ego, which constantly gets in the way of our soul's success. It's one of the things we all must master while here. The core reason to being able to connect with your Spirit team is not for the sake of being shown what's in store for your future. It is to be able to pick up on the daily guidance given to you to make sounder choices that lead you towards what you desire. They'll help you in steps to get there, but they're not going to drop those desires into your lap freely. These guides are within reach for the sake of picking up on those action steps required by you.

Even if you are able to psychically connect with Heaven, it doesn't mean your future will be relayed to you. Connecting with your team is not for fortune telling purposes. In fact, that's one of the last things on their list for wanting you to be able to have a stronger connection with them. Your Spirit team of Guides and Angels do not live your life for you. What is conveyed is on a need to know basis that will enrich and grow your soul. They may relay advice that might be displeasing to you, such as living a healthier lifestyle and to exercise more. Some may not want to hear that, but your Spirit team knows that when you are physically healthier, then this equates to a stronger mind and soul. This combo is what also gives you immense reservoirs of energy to stay focused on fulfilling your purposes and goals. They might urge one to exercise because they feel that you'll need energy and clarity for the bigger desire they want to bring you down the line. Every person on the planet is being guided by at least one guide and angel, but that soul is also being pulled in another direction by the Darkness energies that rule and penetrate the Earth in a darker part of the spirit world that is separate from Heaven.

Every soul is communicating with the Other Side whether they're aware of it or not. I walk from my car to the elevators in a corporate building and Spirit messages are sifting through me mostly via clairaudience (clear hearing) or claircognizance (clear knowing). I'm not doing anything specific to make it happen. Nor am I attempting to conduct a psychic reading. I'm not asking my Spirit team questions as I walk hurriedly to my destination. On an hour to hour basis the messages naturally fall into my vicinity without me wanting or thinking about it. I was born with heightened psychic abilities that were bouncing off the charts by the time I was four. I've forever had one foot in this world and the other in the spirit world. It wasn't something developed over time or over an interest in the spiritual world. It's been this way for as long as I can remember. This is one of the reasons as to why I'm a neurotic all over the place mess at times picking up on every shred of nuance around me.

Some people connect with their Spirit team as naturally as you brush your teeth. Others struggle to pick up on messages or they feel they're receiving nothing. Your Spirit team never disappears or stops communicating with you. When you feel you are receiving nothing, then there could be a block in your life that you might be unaware of or your vibration energy has dropped. What lowers your vibration is also a block. It can be any negative feeling experienced, which is connected to your mind. It can be a particular bad food you ingest, which is connected to your body. Poor diets weigh you down over time. It darkens your aura colors and creates a layer of dirt particles that can only be seen by Heaven or a Clairvoyant, which is connected to your soul. An exaggerated entertaining image of this is the character *Pig-Pen* from the Charlie Brown cartoon moving about with the cloud of dust around him.

When you ingest a diet primarily of toxins, then the toxins become you. This contributes to blocking incoming messages from spirit. When you eat chemically processed foods on a regular basis, then this energy infuses itself into your soul. Think about what kinds of food might have existed at the beginning of humankind and you have a pretty good idea of what is okay to consume. It was over time that humankind began heavily processing foods with unnecessary chemicals, additives, and fats. Junk food didn't exist at the beginning of time. Eating a healthy diet of fruits and vegetables is what assists greatly in removing psychic spirit blocks. It is also awesome for your mental and physical health, your soul and physical body. None of the content we're going to discuss in this book should be taken as condemnation or judgment. It's about being more mindful about making sounder choices to improve your state of well-being by how you think, feel, and what you put in your body. When it comes to toxic foods and drinks that you love, then view those favorite guilty pleasure toxins to be used in moderation if you're unable to let go of it.

Not all toxic foods will create a psychic spirit block since everyone's physical and mental chemistry is complex. We're rattling off the potential basics that could be blocking someone from connecting with Spirit while weighing their energy and life force down.

It's okay to indulge once in a random while. My weakness in my early twenties was Pizza and Beer. As I changed and leaned more towards a healthier diet my cravings for Pizza and Beer were reduced to next to nothing, which means I don't crave it anymore. I'm not opposed to it, but my tastes and palette have changed. You train your palette to become used to what you're eating whether it's good or bad for you. If something tastes weird that's good for you, then it won't be long before you become accustomed to the taste where it doesn't bother you so much. It wasn't much of a fight when I began juicing cucumbers in my twenties. It's like drinking water where I can feel the nutrients spread out through my body every time I drink it. I had my first sip of carrot juice when I was seventeen. I made a weird face, but I kept drinking it because I knew it was good for me. It didn't take long before I craved carrot juice and I ended up loving the taste and have been drinking it regularly since.

One of the big ways of connecting with Spirit is by raising your vibration. Someone that partakes in fortune telling readings or is gifted with psychic foresight could have a low vibration or operate from their ego, but they are still able to connect effortlessly. Raising your vibration is much more important in doing beyond reasons of being more psychic. You pick up on heavenly messages when your ego steps out of the way of your higher self. Meditating and being in a still environment in nature is a great way to access Spirit much easier than when you're under stress or any other negative emotion. This raises your vibration and opens up your psychic clair channels, which also gives you more mental alertness and stamina.

Your vibration is an invisible energy field within the DNA of your soul, aura, and body. The ones able to see that the energy is not invisible are those in Heaven. An Earthly soul with dominate clairvoyance can see the energy field as well. A clairsentient will be able to feel this energy. The vibration energy is a part of you. It is made up of undetectable cells by the human eye that fluctuate and change colors depending on your mood, your thought processes, who you surround yourself with, as well as what you ingest into your body. Your soul and entire aura is an everlasting breathing energy field that has an effect on your state of mind. This is whether you desire to be happy in this life or miserable.

You can be a CEO that is a perpetual angry curmudgeon rude to the staff and only interested in making money in any way they can. This person might be financially successful, but they are spiritually bankrupt. Spiritual soul power has far greater beneficial force than finances in the end. An angry state lowers their vibration, which brings in an onslaught of negative circumstances and harsh health issues at some point in their life. This is due to the angry stressed state they've endured throughout the course of their human existence. It builds up like mold in a damp basement until the individual decides to eradicate it and make some healthy lifestyle changes. Many don't bother until they receive a major health scare that could result in death according to their Doctor. This shakes that person out of the way they had been living. Don't wait until later in life to receive a scare to snap into taking care of yourself. If angry business people worked on well-being exercises, then this would help them be more in tune, which assists them in building their business to even greater success. In fact, I've conversed with many business executives that have admitted to me that they consult the Tarot on occasion for certain decision making.

You are in a temporary physical body with an inflated ego that pushes you to anger or sadness when life circumstances throw you a curve ball. This can be inevitable depending on the kind of life you live and who you surround yourself with. You could be a busy professional that works a job that drains your soul's life force. Working a job you despise will lower your vibration. It's been said that there are a whopping 70% of people that hate their jobs. You sit in traffic to get to this job you're unhappy at only to leave at the end of the day and sit in traffic to get home. This stress in driving in those conditions lowers your vibration. This is why it's vital to incorporate some fun in your life at least one to two times a week. Take frequent breaks throughout the day that include getting outside to breathe in some fresh air. Heavens messages travel along the particles of oxygen that invigorates your life force.

The fun you inject can be whatever lightens your load. It can be getting together with a friend to go to a restaurant to hang out and shoot the breeze. It can be heading off to the beach or to go on a hike in nature. It can be watching a funny movie or playing a board game. It can be date night with your lover or releasing tension at the gym in a workout. Spirit won't point the finger and tell you not to drink a six-pack of beer to lighten that load. That's something only you can decide. Drinking a six pack lowers your vibration and you wake up feeling even more rundown. I know because I've been in that state myself. I was one of those party animals when I was twenty-one, which is so hard to believe today. I would have a drink, but then counterbalance it with one of my cucumber or carrot concoctions.

Every living organism, plant, animal, element, atom, and cell vibrates of energy. When you take a stroll through a garden or park, you'll notice an invisible heavy weight being lifted off you. You suddenly start to feel elated and more relaxed. This is an example of what it might feel like as your vibration begins to rise. But then you get a phone call from a friend who is a gossip and proceeds to tell you about how someone you both know did something and they angrily disapprove. Now your vibration begins to decline even though you didn't do anything, but answer your phone. You were on the receiving end absorbing the negative energy that your friend was outwardly shooting at your soul. Now your vibration has dropped down.

Some animals will dart away when they sense a hostile energy coming towards them. They're highly in tune that they guard their territory without thinking about it. The reason most animals have high vibrations is because they do not live the kinds of lives that human folk live. They're not stressing out over making money to pay rent. They're not thinking about where their next meal is coming from. When they're hungry they will seek it out at that point. They're not falling into emotional turmoil because a lover has left them. They eat, breathe, move, go to the bathroom, sleep, and then repeat.

A pet of an abusive owner will have a dropped vibration. If the animal has been trained by the owner to feel fear due to the poor abuse of that human owner, then the fear emotion drops the animals' vibration. Human souls are responsible for the havoc and destruction that happens on this planet. They're responsible for the harm done to people, animals, planet life, and so on. The other exception is Mother Nature. The weather on the planet can be uncontrollable and erratic in places. It can and will destroy anything in its wake. Earth can thrive and prosper rapidly without humankind tampering with everything.

The astrological sign of Pisces is considered one of the most psychic signs in the zodiac, because like the symbol of the fish they are born absorbing every nuance naturally. Like a fish in the water, when you attempt to get close to someone with Pisces in the top tier of their chart that person will evade or swim away. You have to keep at them if you truly care to ensure they know you're safe to be around. Feeling every nuance causes heavy burden on the backs of the Pisces. They can be prone to addictions to hard substances just to get rid of that feeling. When they evolve and become more aware that it is a gift and not a curse, then they can reach greater heights than anyone has ever dreamed of. We're using the sign of the Pisces as an example in order to demonstrate what it's like for someone who might have strong sensitivities and how they might navigate through life. This is regardless of what someone's sign is. Will it be addicted? Or will they choose to soar high above the clouds in spiritual transcendence?

When you welcome the hostile energy in someone else, then you become one with it. Becoming one with it is when you engage with someone that has hostile energy. This also includes engaging with hostile people on social media.

As I moved through my twenties, I grew to have a zero-tolerance policy for negativity of any kind. This means I'd cut out those that were perpetually negative. This isn't about not being a listening ear to the occasional negative experience a friend is having. This is about the offenders that reside in a 24/7 ordeal that is filled with constant complaints and negativity. There is zero positivity that rarely peeks out. They have no interest in shifting that mind set or taking steps to make positive changes in their life. When you move into that sort of negative state, then you've officially moved into the state of victimhood. You have the power to change your life by the will of your own thoughts. This is by seeing the good that is working for you more than the challenges. It is seeing the blessings rather than what you don't have. My entire spirit being repels negativity because the cells of my soul open up and drink that in, which is not a comfortable feeling. It's easier to rip that negativity out immediately rather than be tortured by it.

You might have a complicated life and therefore live in ways that are not conducive to raising one's vibration. Perhaps it's at a cutthroat stressed out environment at your job or with your home life. This is about being aware of what can and will lower your vibration while doing your best to avoid the negatives when possible. When your mind is consciously aware of what you need to do even when you're not doing it, then this is a step in the right direction. It becomes second nature to you as you adopt healthier life changes.

My most toxic addicted years were in my late teens to early twenties. I was drinking tons of alcohol, doing lines of cocaine, meth, smoking cigarettes, and marijuana regularly. As I was doing that, I was consciously aware in the back of my mind that if I'm not going to stop at that moment, then I better incorporate some healthy lifestyle choices. I'd do a line of cocaine and chase it down with carrot juice. This lasted until I started following my Spirit team's repetitive shouting guidance in my clairaudient ear that I needed to stop. I was listening to them during that time, but I was ignoring them like a spoiled child ignoring his parent's naggings. This was primarily during my rebellious punk years of the late teens to early twenties, which is pretty common for many around that age. It's when parents worry about their child the most, especially if they're as out of control as I was.

My Spirit team has always been igniting my inner life force to the point where I would crave toxic vices less to complete elimination of the toxic addiction. I knew I needed to stop with much of it, so I eventually folded and requested their help in doing so. It was after admitting that I needed their help did they infuse me with the discipline to do so. Alcohol in high amounts lowers your vibration, which I don't think is too much of a surprise to many. This does not mean that they are demanding that you stop drinking. Your choices to do, stop, dissolve, or reduce particular life choices that drop your vibration is for you to decide. If you enjoy drinking a bottle of wine every night and yet you regularly question why you're not content with your life, and nothing ever goes your way, then this would be one of the possibilities as to what is blocking what you desire from entering the picture. Since alcohol in high amounts blocks the divine and lowers your vibration, then you miss out on the messages and guidance from your own Spirit team. Having a drink once in a while is not going to kill you. This is about the repetitive regular abuse of toxins.

Some of the common messages and guidance I've received from Heaven are geared towards the importance of exercise and taking care of all things connected to your body. I've been into physical activity since I was a kid thanks to the urging of my Spirit team. Even when I fell off the wagon and into heavy toxic addictions, such as drugs, cigarettes, and alcohol as a late teen and young adult, I was still greatly aware of the importance of taking care of myself in the back of my mind. My Spirit team dominated my need to destroy my body and got me back into shape by focusing strongly on my overall well-being by the time I was twenty-five years old.

Raising your vibration is a lifestyle change that positively benefits your soul and all aspects of your life. There are values that need to be adopted or modified in order to reach a centered place that helps you be more connected. This carries over beyond what you're consuming and into what you're feeling and thinking. If you spend months obsessing over an ex-lover that is no longer in your life, then this is a block that lowers your vibration.

This ex has left you, moved on, or perhaps blocked you on social media or on a phone app with no explanation, yet you cannot find a way to let it go and move on, then this lowers your vibration keeping it there until you permanently extricate the ex from your aura. You are checking your ex's social media page regularly to see what they're up to. Are there signs they might be interested in you again? Who are they talking to? What photos do they post with other people in them? Could they be romantically or sexually connected to any of the people in the photos? What about those who comment on your ex's posts? Is something going on with your ex and that commenter?

Your ego is running the show that is your life. It is desperately curious to know or find out some clues about what's going on with this ex-lover. This lowers your vibration and creates a block. If someone is no longer interested in communicating with you, then that is your cue to work on moving on and walking away. I understand this as I've been there too. It's not something that happens overnight, and some people have a harder time letting go. The moment you visit this person's social media page to spy and read their posts with the intention of discovering new information that can benefit you, then your vibration drops. This isn't about checking a friend's page to see what they've been posting lately to find out what they're up to because you've been busy with work, school, or any other life activity. You don't have any emotional interest except genuine positive feelings to stay up to date on your friend's life. That will likely not lower your vibration unless you read a tirade of negative posts from them.

A low vibration is what makes you depressed, miserable, angry, or agitated. When you focus heavily on this ex, talking about them, focusing on it, and wondering, then this drops your vibration. Your vibration continues to drop whenever you obsess over their every move.

When you're still checking up on them months after they left you, then that's when it may be time to look at taking action steps to cut it all loose for your benefit. Talk to a counselor, therapist, healer, or join a support group and get outdoors more and connect with friends. Find ways to muster up the effort to continue on with life without the ex that left. It will be a struggle, but overtime it will get easier. The thoughts of them will dissolve gradually to the point where it's only once in a while. When they do pop into your mind here and there after you've healed, then the emotional quotient surrounding the thoughts and feelings won't be as intense as they once were. You can think of them the way you do anyone you were once close to.

It's natural to be going through all of those feelings, thoughts, and emotions after a breakup, but eventually you do it less as time progresses on.

If you don't move through the grieving emotions, then after a year of this you'll find that it has ultimately destroyed your life force. This includes your work, friendships, overall soul's well-being, and creative pursuits to name a few. It stalls circumstances until you begin the process of re-raising your vibration again and getting back to that place of perfect contentment. You will get there with effort and discipline. It's a gradual progression as you deal with the death of what no longer is in your life to make room for what is. Your interest in the coming and goings of others will decline. You'll notice improvement and positive changes happening steadily as a result.

When your vibration is low it takes effort and work to re-raise it. You can raise it when you decide to move swiftly through making important positive life changes and adjustments to reach a place where you're content again. Somebody who is no longer a part of your current life is not your higher self's priority or concern. You begin to think of them less while diving into living life again.

Take frequent breaks and disconnect from technology and/or hostile people in order to re-center and gain perspective. Sometimes the most in tune person can be too close to the truth to pick up on it. Letting loose in a joyful hobby releases your soul from the clutches of the burdens of the body. It raises your vibration in the process. There isn't enough fun in people's lives these days and so this is much needed.

When you tune into your guides energy, write down any great ideas or dreams you've been thinking of no matter how big or small. It can be positive behavior changes and perspectives you want to begin incorporating into your soul make up. This is guidance being passed down to you in some fashion by your Spirit team. They might instruct you to make a pact to have weekend getaways at least once a month or every two months. It can be a business plan or asking someone out on a date. Incorporate these lifestyle adjustments one-step at a time and notice the positive effects that end up coming out of that.

CHAPTER TWO

*Fire Up
Your Inner Child*

You grow older, your body ages, and you become more hip to the idea that you need to be responsible and disciplined if you want to survive living on the planet as pain free as possible. You have bills to pay, clothes to buy, and food to eat. How far in before you've lost yourself in physical Earthly demands?

You know you're beginning to lose yourself when your relationships with those around you grow distant or fall apart. It's when you find that you've been running on empty, stressed, tired, or all of the above. The way human life is today is that you cannot permanently sit on the couch all day drinking beer, app chatting, and texting. You need to get a job, have larger goals, make money, live life, and support yourself. You'll want to keep a fine line between doing that and not losing yourself to the point where your inner child is trapped until its release when you pass on.

Your inner child is the person you were before age ten. It is the innocent all loving part of you as a child that had no judgment or criticisms of other people. Those criticisms came upon you through your environment and at the hands of those who heavily influenced you. If you grew up in a community where the people were racist, then the chances of you developing this racism trait are higher than anyone else. You were not born racist and nor were you prejudice against anyone and their life choices. This goes for any sort of bias from political affiliations, religion, or hatred of someone's sexual orientation. None of that exists with your inner child.

Your inner child is the part of you that has the strongest access to God. It is the part of you that is in an all-encompassing state of love, joy, and peace knowing how to stop judging and thinking negative thoughts and just have fun. The inner child longs for this release if only your ego would pull that part of you back out to play again. When the dark ego dominates and grows lost in the physical world, your inner child screams for attention and love. Diving into creative artistic pursuits is a great way to fire up your inner child. When your inner child remains buried under rubble, then feelings of emptiness and loss begin to rise. Some go through these feelings of being lost during pinnacle times in their life. It can be brought upon due to a loss of any kind. This might be the loss of a job, a friendship, a lover, or any other loss to something that gave you a sense of security or happiness.

Lost feelings for a prolonged period of time can also indicate that you're moving through a transition that will eventually lead to an awakening. This awakening is where you gain clarity on everything around you and what you need to do. There is no time limit when moving through a transition or a personal evolution. It can take one month, one year, or three years. Allow what is intended to evolve without interference. Go about life's business and avoid pushing for anything to happen in a stressed-out haze.

Your inner child is who you were before all of the layers of trauma and life experiences jaded you. It was when you saw life without judgment or critique. You saw life through the lens of pure innocence and love. It was before human tampering made you despise anyone different from you. Those who despise someone that is different we're not that way when they were four years old. It was their caregivers, peers, community, and societies influence that taught all of that stuff. If God raised you, then you would've grown up to see the love in all souls. You would exude love and joy full time. Seeing the love in all souls means psychically peering beneath their hardened cold and unkind exterior to see who they were at birth.

When you were born you were immensely psychic, and filled with overflowing feelings of love, joy, and peace. You were wide eyed ready to absorb everything around you. You saw the beauty in life, in the colors, and in the trees. You were also a sponge absorbing the environment you were growing up in.

If your parents were the type that would constantly argue with one another in front of you, then this hostile energy is absorbed and becomes a part of your consciousness. If your caregivers and the society you live in were prejudice in any form, then this rubs off on you and you begin to believe this is the way it is. If someone is different from you, then you are automatically repulsed by them. Hate is not something you were born with, but your environment, society, and peers teach this to you. It adds another layer around your inner child until there are so many layers that your inner child is trapped within unable to get your attention.

The souls that enter into this life from the various realms in Heaven are born into an Earthly life for a bigger purpose. They evolve at a rapid pace than a newborn soul would. They're the ones that might grow up in a toxic environment, but have higher awareness and psychic intuition to know that the way everyone else is behaving or thinking doesn't seem to have any balance in it. The realm soul might be considered the black sheep of the family, or the outcast, or weird. You are and always will be a child of God with a greater purpose than perhaps someone having their first Earthly life run.

You may have a growing adult body, but inside this physical case beneath all of the layers of your experiences resides your inner child. Your inner child is buried underneath an avalanche of experiences, lifestyle choices, and human development interference. When you had a negative, toxic, or abusive experience, then this is seared into your consciousness even if you continue on with life having great times. This child within you cries out for fun whenever you're feeling any negative emotion. Your inner child is psychic always operating from a higher vibration than any other part of you. This is why Heaven urges others to find that part of you and bring them back out. Your inner child is pure joy to be around, so let this part of you run free once in a while in order to bring you back.

Energy Drainers

Energy draining people and lifestyle choices suffocated one's inner child. Have a zero-tolerance policy for any meanness, negativity, or drama from anyone. There is a difference between loving someone from afar without getting caught up in their drama or toxic energy, to choosing to keep them at arm's length if you don't want them to go away. It might be a family member, parent, sibling, friend, or colleague. It can be someone that is seemingly not easy to deal with, so you cut them out of your life permanently if possible. You love the goodness in them, but no one should put themselves in a position where they are a punching bag which affects your self-esteem and your ever-growing consciousness.

Someone might not be mean towards you directly, but they harshly complain about other people to you. This causes you to end up feeling down or worn out after communicating with them. Having your energy drained by others is real. This is why those on the receiving end grow weakened, annoyed, or rubbed the wrong way. Those doing the energy draining are not necessarily aware they are, because this type of energy makes one clouded.

You can be an exceptionally good compassionate person yourself and not realize when you're in the midst of behaving in a negative way. You're having a physical human experience and it's going to happen once in a while. You want to be aware of that when it happens. This is about someone that is always negative or toxic every time you connect with them.

When negative energy from someone else is around you, then you want to steer clear of it and not become consumed by it. If you drown in it, then this will bring you down, darken your aura, and lower your vibration. All of these phrases mean the same thing. If you are a sensitive or in tune to energies beyond the physical world, then you cannot deny how it makes you feel when you're around someone toxic. You can have love for them and still choose to not engage with them full time. Connect with them in small doses and then wrap it up and excuse yourself that you need to leave. They might react in a tantrum, but don't fall into guilt. You have to think of you first.

Everyone is living their own path, and no one

can live it for them. If someone chooses to head down a self-destructive path, then no one can stop them. They have to want to change on their own. You can be polite when they reach out to you, but blow in and out of there quickly. This way they're not around long enough to infiltrate your area with their toxins.

The key is to say, "I have love for them and wish them well, but we don't engage much. When we do, I stand in a place of emotional detachment."

Energy draining is a major issue in the lives of millions of people around the world. It pushes them to pop pills to sleep, or pop them to wake up to continue on. It lures them into toxic addictions such as alcohol, food, and even drugs. You can wake up feeling alive and joyful, then you get in your car to head to work and the traffic is so bad that by the time you arrive at work you feel drained and dejected. The planet is overflowing with people and so many of them understand the fight to keep on going everyday morning and night. Others underestimate how bad traffic can be when they find a job and a place to live. You might think you live fifteen minutes away from work, but that is until you neglect to consider that the commute can be thirty to forty minutes. And that's on a good day! This is a major energy drainer and so are some of the choices one makes in their life. This can be from who you associate with from friendships to love relationships. Working with one bad apple can spoil your work life.

When you notice these circumstances happening, then you want to begin the process of considering the options you can make to alleviate this kind of stress. What areas can you change today and what areas will take longer than that. You do not want to spend years in a situation that drains your energy since this is equal to draining your life force. Not to mention the long-term health issues that can arise, and the blocks erected between yourself and Heaven's guidance.

Hugging and Touching

Hugging and touching have immense healing properties to the soul. It awakens your inner child, which is also connected to the creative part of you. Are you overworked, stressed, depressed, or angry? Hug others more and allow them to hug you. Hugging lowers your blood pressure, relieves stress, and releases the brain chemical Oxytocin. This contributes to positive bonding or otherwise known as the love hormone. Hugging reminds you that we're all on the same side. Many of the cure all remedies for so many issues reside within you. Hugs are one of the various activities that promote positive health. And hugs don't cost anything. They're free!

Naturally, you're not going to randomly approach a stranger or someone at work to hug them out of nowhere since that would be inappropriate. Hugging is with those you know personally that won't be bothered by it otherwise ask, "Can I hug you?"

Of course, they might say, "What? No. Why

are you acting weird?"

They're not used to that kind of affection as it was absent during crucial moments in their growing up phase that they came to expect unkindness.

There was this story of a straight male father that went to a gay pride festivity wearing a shirt or t-shirt that said, "Free hugs". Random people were going up to hug him. He recalled feeling their emotion from one guy to another girl that wouldn't let go. He could sense they hadn't been loved in so long by anyone. They were likely thrown out of the house or ostracized from their family for being gay. The man acted as an angel to say, "I love you and you are accepted."

It's not like someone that needs to be hugged is going to go up to a total stranger to ask if they can hug them. People end up wandering life jaded, stressed, or feeling unloved when all they need to bring their soul back out is that hug. If you're willing to part with a hug, then do it more often. Hug your friend, your lover, and even your pet! Unless your pet is a goldfish, then you can just pucker up and blow kisses at it from the glass of the aquarium. Animals are souls and crave the hug of another. Hugging is one of the many great vibration enhancers. For a brief moment your soul can breathe while in the midst of a hug. It tears away any off-putting ions that latch itself onto the aura around your spirit. You experience release and you understand what freedom feels like.

Everyone needs a hug whether they like to admit it or not. The most toughened human soul needs that love to tear down the walls they've built around their heart. You've likely come across someone who you try to hug and they clam up or turn into a brick wall with harms falling to the side barely giving back a hug in return, or they give you that police pat on the shoulder during the hug, "Alright, alright, let's not get goofy now."

They're terribly uncomfortable being touched as it's not something they likely grew up getting enough of. They hardened over time at some point in their life.

Many are angry, depressed, or feeling any other kind of emotion that disconnects your soul from a feeling of joy, peace, or love. Those qualities are traits which are innate inside of you, but buried so far deep it can't climb out of the hole it's trapped itself in. The world needs a war on hugs. If you're going to complain about something, then complain that you're not receiving enough love, hugs, and kisses from the world. There are millions of nerve endings in the human skin and to experience touch activates these nerves prompting you to raise your vibration releasing your inner child out of its caged prison within you.

Bring on the Joy

Joy is one of the highest vibrating energies that exist next to love. When someone laughs into hysterics, you sense the infectious energy. Suddenly strangers around that person light up with a smile. Someone else's energy will affect others around them. If they're being negative, then that will transfer. If they're infectiously giggly, then that will transfer. Seeing the fun and lightheartedness in situations raises your vibration. It lightens the heavy loaded burdens of stress. When your vibration is high, you attract in brighter circumstances to you. If you're stuck in negative feelings, then call upon your Spirit team and ask them to help in elevating your soul into a happier space. Request they guide you to getting back into the joy of your life again. Radiating with joy is what brings more of that good stuff to you. No one wants to be around a miserable stressed out and depressed grump. Feeling joy while visualizing your desires is what helps the manifestation process take place more quickly too. Archangel Jophiel is the hierarchy angel to call on to bring more joy and beauty into your life.

The working class is breaking their back to put food on the table and take care of their families and loved ones. They're being run ragged into the ground. This is thanks to human decision to work people like dogs. I've had so many conversations with the working class over the years and I've heard their common understandable complaints. I wonder how many politicians have truly heard the stories I have or even care. If they have, then they would've implemented change by now.

I'm an advocate for hard work as are the beings in Heaven, but this means working hard while incorporating regular time outs to decompress and spend with your loved ones. This isn't about working one day a month while doing nothing the rest of the time. This is working smarter schedules.

Although the five-day forty-hour work week is excessive, it was much worse pre-1900's when people were expected to work ten to sixteen hours a day. Soon it was realized that it needed to be cut shorter, so they implemented the weekend off to give people a break.

Now even that's not enough since lives are busier than ever. People are getting smarter and hip to the fact that the soul and body need more adequate time for rest and relaxation. It's currently not enough, because by the time the weekend comes around people spend the first day getting all of that practical stuff they did not have time to get done during the week. The second and last day is spent burned out lounging around. Finally, on the third day they're energetic and ready to do something fun, but alas it's time to head back into work.

At least several times a month incorporate playtime and personal time. This is essential to your overall health and wellbeing. This will also increase productivity and decrease health issues, not to mention help the crumbling of relationship connections. This personal time isn't used to go grocery shopping, gassing up the car, or gym time, which is a necessity and wasted on one of the weekend days off. It's to connect with loved ones, relax, rejuvenate, take a day trip, or any other fun activity that helps you let go and release.

Heaven watches millions of people rushing to and from a job burned out and running on little sleep. It saddens them to have this aerial view of so many detached souls that are unhappy deep down.

It's no wonder there is a rise in disconnection from God. Heaven demands that all souls take a time out to enjoy regular bouts of personal luxury time. When you include fun and relaxation in your life, then when you head back to work, you're more energetic and focused. Your soul is crying out in pain when it runs on any permanent negative emotion. Stress, anxiety, and depression are examples of symptoms that crush your soul. This energy shoots into your physical body causing an array of issues. It also merges into your aura and touches other people's auras around you that absorb that.

Luxuries are a necessity for your soul so that it can be awakened out of its cold corporate prison that life circumstances have created around it. Let your inner child out and have fun once in a while. Shake off the seriousness and the constant critical gossip and judgments of other people and circumstances.

CHAPTER THREE

Nature Therapy

Improving your psychic senses simultaneously improves your spiritual connection with the Divine. Some find anything connected to psychic phenomena as being of the Devil, but the irony is having a strong connection with God comes through your psychic senses that everyone is born with including the non-believers or strictly religious. Some strict religious groups that disapprove of psychic behavior will talk about having a godly vision or that they prayed on something that helped. Where do you think that communication is coming from? It's coming through your psychic senses. Some might strongly disagree with something and call it evil without having any knowledge of it enough to be making a comment. That's been going on since the dawn of humanity. They may be confusing the possibility that having a strong psychic antenna can invite in negative spirits. Negative spirits will attack whoever they can get close to, including a non-believer, a believer, or someone psychically in tune, so that theory is null and void. There are also numerous cases of a dark spirit attaching itself to a devout religious follower, so the belief that a dark spirit can only be conjured up by a Medium also isn't bathed in truth.

Strengthening your psychic clair senses helps with increasing your faith and being able to follow the guidance coming in from above. Getting out into a nature setting can assist the soul in reaching a higher level of awakening. It is far easier for Spirit to access someone when they're in a calming environment such as a nature setting. Many purport to feeling much calmer after taking a stroll in nature. I'm a fan of all things connected to nature, which includes the deserts and badlands with its dry terrain and extensive geological erosions that cast into a breathtaking color display of volcanic rock, canyons, and mesas. Those areas have always proven great escapes to commune with my higher council through the winds as the sage Native American Wise Ones once did in massive numbers across North America. All that remains are the clues left behind in entombed sediments of extinct fossils of tribal skulls and dinosaur-like creatures that no longer roam the Earth, but whose presence is profoundly felt.

Spirit communication travels along the particles of oxygen, so where there is wind there is spirit in grave numbers. It gives you an opportunity for reflection, redemption, and answers. Just like Bob Dylan said in his song, "The answer my friend is blowing in the wind."

The Divine answers are travelling along with the wind. The sense of time while in those nature places is what hits you. You realize we have a short shelf lifespan. You hear that from others of older age that it flies by, so take advantage of the time you have while here. As a teenager at a party, I was conversing with this woman in her thirties. I still remember her saying, "Make your choices today. I wish I knew then what I know now."

What she said forever stuck for me because I knew what she was talking about. I knew that a human life glides by faster than you would believe while in your teens and twenties, so don't waste one minute not getting into life's work and diving into your purpose. Otherwise you'll wake up one day and look in the mirror and wonder where the time went. I remember being in panicked mode around age fifteen and sixteen realizing that I need to get moving and get to work as my life is flying by. I was hyper aware as a teenager of what was up ahead while here. I've talked to people that reach older age when it truly hits them. They were young and vibrant with the whole world at their feet. After years of disappointments, what they once dreamed of seemed to grow impossible and unlikely to transpire. They may look their age, but inside feel as if they're still sixteen. Continue to expand your mind and consciousness beyond the routine, so that you can take advantage of every moment while here.

There are various reasons I love all nature power places. It offers quiet contemplation through Divine spirit connecting. It also gives you an injection of clarity along with a wider perspective that can easily get lost when you fall into the superficiality or the mundane of physical life.

When I was twenty years old, I knew those shallow interests were great for five minutes, but I needed to be challenged. I was a sponge screaming inside for more than what people gave me through Earthly patterns. There was no way I could endure living with a mediocre mindset, even if that meant I would be set apart from everyone else, which I was regardless.

In vast nature settings, your view broadens and opens up. You see who you are in comparison to this temporary home of a planet. Things like social media suddenly seem trivial in contrast. All of the wrangling on it does nothing to attract any kind of a positive abundant mindset, but instead dulls the spirit senses, your life force, and vibrational energy unless you are using it for good and positivity. Living hypnotized by the toxic allure and superficial triviality gossip every second can be depressing. Some believe it's natural to remain in a superficial state, because it's what's taught. Some of it might arguably be fun once in a while, but to endure that indefinitely can be primitively medieval.

Have faith and believe what you desire will come and that you are deserving of good. Be open and receptive to receive ensure you're balancing giving and receiving energy throughout your life. This is by not overdoing one without the other. This imbalance can block the positive movement flow. Examine what your desires are and what work you're willing to put in to achieve your goals.

Act and be persistent with it. Helping the movement along positively means putting in the work. Kicking back dreaming of desires to come to fruition doesn't help those desires come to life. Dreaming of desires is a great first step to take. It's the dreams in your mind and visions that start out like a seed. These dreams gradually begin to develop in your mind for a while, much like a human pregnancy until that moment when you give birth to your dreams, as if you're giving birth to a child. Once that happens, you initiate action steps that can help the dreams grow and evolve.

Have a plan and know what you want, so as not to confuse the positive attraction quotient. Take regular time outs, retreats, and vacations. This helps alleviate stress, opens your psychic clair senses, and brings great ideas in. It helps elevate your vibration since people tend to be in a brighter spirit when they take a break. Study, perfect, and expand your mind and consciousness. All of this helps in cracking open the door to abundance.

CHAPTER FOUR

*Elevating Your Mind,
Body, and Spirit*

God, Spirit, and the Divine's energy moves through me in waves. I, and you, are one with God. From as far back as eight years old, I could feel His energy pushing me forward to take care of myself on all levels from the mind, body, and soul spirit. From as minor as going for a jog or a bike ride to delving my mind into study and learning. Since my childhood years, fitness and exercise have forever been a big part of my life's interests without ever fading.

I can remember teaching myself to learn to ride a bike the same way I'd teach myself to do anything and everything I was interested in. We couldn't afford much growing up, so when one of my childhood friends went out of town, he left me his bike to practice with. It was diving into the practice, which helped me to teach myself to ride a bike. There was no one walking me through the steps. The Internet and You Tube instructional videos didn't exist in those days. I grabbed the bike and practiced on my own. I fell off it a number of times, but I picked myself up, picked the bike up, and continued on with the persistent practice until by the time my friend came back, I was an excellent bike rider. This is how I trained myself to do anything and everything I had a desire to learn. It was through the avenue of tough no-nonsense streets smarts and practice that would carry with me throughout my Earthly life.

I learned things through the school of hard knocks. This was by jumping on in and doing the work without any formal training. Due to my inhibiting ADD/ADHD, learning anything was fraught with some kind of disability anyway. I couldn't retain by sitting in a class listening to a lecture. I had to dive in and actually do the work.

Since I was a teenager, the major jobs I received throughout my life consisted of me being the candidate with zero experience for the job being interviewed for. In the end, I was the candidate they went with. I was able to convince them I could excel at whatever it was they gave me. I might be rusty at first, but give me a few trial runs and they will be unable to find a harder worker that can master it over someone with the education and experience. It was this passion coupled with my forthright fighting nature that was my winning card.

This proved true as many of those employers later commented long after I left the employment that they chose well when taking that risk to go with the person without the credentials or experience only to be blown away. These employers that remained in contact with me long after I left all had informed me they were unable to find a suitable replacement that could do what I did for them.

The point of that is that it has been my long running mantra throughout life. Be a fighter in all you do. Have passion, persistence, drive, and a strong will to do the job fast and fearless. I've always had an interest in being completely aware, conscious, and driven to be the best I can be. My interest and focus on expanding my mind, strengthening my body, and nourishing my soul were present since childhood. I've persistently been a huge promoter of taking care of yourself on all levels. This advocacy includes the body through fitness, exercise, and nutrition.

Even when I fell into my young adult party days of alcohol, drugs, and cigarettes in my early twenties, I was still conscious enough to work out hard if I was going to be putting those toxins in my body. Luckily, the partying days evaporated by the time I was moving into my mid-to-late twenties. My main focus moved right into fitness and exercise in a broader way. I knew that a strong body was necessary. This had nothing to do with vanity, which is why some work out. There has been evidence that some people work out and take care of themselves more while single, but as soon as they end up in a long-term relationship, they get lazy about it. This is because they were working out to attract someone in rather than working out because they care about their overall well-being. My desire to exercise and work out regularly is partially because I always feel incredible afterwards. If I was feeling low or depressed, I would go for a run or endure a rigorous work out. Suddenly I was feeling stronger and more alive than I had ever been!

The stronger I grew through physical fitness; the stronger my Divine psychic connections became. It also helped me make it through the long days of juggling my day job work life to building my side business life purpose career.

I run into people today and many have commented, "You are so fit!" Never mind the positive side effect that it helps you look good, but what's more important is that I feel incredible! Today I've been told by younger friends that I run circles around them as well as those two to three times younger than I.

This isn't about being better than anyone else, but about motivating others to do the same and push yourself beyond the limits. You have to care about your body the way you care about other things you have interest in. One cannot neglect that physical vessel you were temporarily gifted with.

There will be a day when I may physically not be able to do certain things. Although, one friend once informed me that he and another friend of ours was in Joshua Tree National Park on a particular occasion. As it was getting dark, they noticed a female figure racing down the rocks from up high. She was incredibly fit racing towards them until she slowed down in front of them. He said she might have been in her sixties when they first noticed her. They talked to her and were surprised to learn that she was in her nineties! She's been doing that exercise for decades and feels great.

My mouth was on the floor, "Wow, that's incredible! I love hearing stories like that. I want to be like that if I'm still around in my nineties."

I received a huge rush of joy and excitement to know that it could be possible. God gave you this temporary body to house your soul so that you may live an Earthly physical human life full of lessons, experiences, blessings, missions and challenges. You have to take care of all parts of your body, mind, and soul. All three of these are what the spiritual genre was comprised of, but that's mainly because these are the important aspects that make up the totality of you.

Some people avoid exercise or express disdain and reach for those potato chips and ice cream day after day feeling even more lethargic than the day before. Many shun study and higher learning while instead trying to find their next conquest to have sex with. Some are surprised by the number of messages I receive from people regularly that send me inappropriate messages, as if I'm just a body to use. One would think you should be flattered. When you have an expanding mind and consciousness, but the intelligence is uninteresting to someone, then that comes off more offensive.

I'm highly aware of what people are interested in because I receive this from them every single week. They only have one thing on their mind. Attempting to have any kind of intellectual deep conversation is met with resistance through their one to two-word answers of disinterest in talking about anything beyond physical pleasure. It's about how quickly can you come here and give it to me, for lack of a better phrase. I've had some friends say in recommendation, "I feel like you need to dumb it down for some people."

It's never been said as an attack or harsh judgment, even though I was initially thrown off. I soon realized it was sage advice. They know having a raised consciousness and higher intelligence level in an Earthly world dominated and ruled by the darkness of ego, the superficial, and shallow can be a lonely place for that soul. This has been a common theme complaint from the spiritually based crowd. Many of them have been raising their consciousness and intelligence through knowledge gaining, study, and experiences. They've found it difficult to relate or connect to others that weren't interested in any of that. Some have disbanded friendships that were no longer on that same path.

On Earth, the more superficial you are, then the more popular you become. The masses love superficiality, shallowness, and a hyper focus on the exterior. They want to see hard young bodies, fancy cars and mansions. It doesn't matter what that person has to say as long as they fit that description. A social media user only needs to post something like that without any caption and it will garner thousands of people giving the thumbs up and applause. This isn't a criticism or judgment, but the current sad reality with the evidence being in plain sight for all to see. I've had discussions of this myself with other spiritual buddies. They've told me that people seem to pay more attention to their spiritual posts when there is a shirtless pic in it, and this is on a spiritually based account. Unfortunately, the reality is that is what sells, which is why I have sometimes done that on occasion. The photo is to get their attention in hopes they will see what's more important than the photo and that is the enlightening verbiage that accompanies it.

Many shun deepening their soul and consciousness through spiritual and religious studies coupled with hard driven life experiences. What good is life if the three components of body, mind, and soul that make up basic healthy survival are ignored and discarded.

Work on making healthier life choices. This includes your diet and drink intake as well as adequate regular exercise, pending you are physically able to. You might be someone physically unable to exercise due to human physical challenges this lifetime. This is not directed to those that cannot physically do it due to a handicap or physical issue. This is directed to those that are capable of physical exercise, but don't want to out of laziness or because they hate it.

When you take care of yourself on all levels, then this has an effect on your overall well-being.

Having a strong well-being has a positive effect on your mood and thoughts. This simultaneously elevates the vibration of both your feelings and thoughts, which makes you a powerful abundance attractor. Joy brings in more joy and sadness bring in more sadness. Which would you like to have?

This isn't saying you're not allowed to have any fun. Having fun is an essential luxury. When you operate in high octane stress mode attending to daily practical matters, then you risk burn out. You also raise your stress levels, which drops your vibration. A low vibration can diminish the potential of attracting in positive blessings and abundance. Perhaps you don't care for the theory that pushes you to be positive and avoid negativity. How many people do you know that are perpetually negative, but are simultaneously attracting in all sorts of positive abundance? I don't know of many cases where that exists. I've heard of more cases where someone is a positive optimistic go-getter and is simultaneously attracting in awesome great things in their life.

Get up off the metaphorical couch and out of a dull mindset and get to work. Create a sanctuary in a private space in your house where you can connect to God and your Spirit team to receive profound insights, messages, and guidance that urge you to make positive changes in your life. Pay attention to these messages and act on them.

If your Spirit team is urging you to get outside and exercise, then follow that advice. They know that when you take care of your body that you become a ferocious Divine communicator that helps you make powerfully positive choices that bring your goals and dreams to fruition. Suddenly the flow of positive abundance and blessings starts to move in your direction. Fitness and exercise breathe new life into your soul. It helps dissolve or reduce any negative emotions such as depression or stress. You feel an uplifting crystal-clear calm focus that enables you to put action into your goals that makes great things happen.

Don't beat yourself up if you find exercise difficult at first. The more you do it, then the easier it gets where it eventually becomes like oxygen to you. If two days have passed and I haven't exercised, then I can feel it in a big way. I can feel it in my body and entire state of being. I can feel it in my psychic senses pushing me to soar forward freely in an exercise routine to re-awaken it. I have to dive on in before I go crazy. I'm then transported into the spirit of the Divine with this essence moving throughout my entire body. Great ideas soon rise to the forefront over what I need to do and accomplish.

Whenever I have an unresolved problem, I go directly to God the ultimate source of guidance. I don't rely on human beings to prop me up and change my life. I rely on God to help prop me up and change my life. He has that power having proven it to me time and again.

It's no one else's job to cheer you up, bring you joy, or lavish you with attention. Stop expecting other people to take on the responsibility of bringing you joy. Avoid being dependent on others to prop you up, fix you, and give you devotion. And stop getting angry when others are not catering to you the way you want them to. Doing that will only result in frustration and bitterness, which is the perfect breeding ground for the Darkness to grow. No one can fulfill that impossible demand. Anyone with any measure of a healthy self-esteem won't stick around and bow down to that kind of energy.

It is your responsibility to create your own joy and prop yourself up. Avoid relying on people to remind you of your worth. Pull yourself up by your bootstraps, stand tall, and know your worth by empowering yourself through Source. When you've excelled at reaching that space where you no longer need or require any of that from others, then does all the good stuff start to fall into place naturally on its own. And even if it doesn't, you could careless as you're not craving validation anyway.

This joy seeking attention from others is more about the co-dependent and toxic like relationships that others rely on. It is not necessarily about the healthier balanced relationships where you feel joy being around your partner as they do with you. There may be some that fall into the space of needing constant attention from others, whether it's from a lover, friends, family members, or strangers. They love messages of joy, but fail to notice when they have been guilty of falling into the co-dependency aspect part of it.

It's sometimes hard to believe that I was once a co-dependent person while in my early twenties. I mistakenly put too much dependence on other people to prop me up and fix me. Luckily, it was only a matter of years in where I rose above it and realized that it wasn't working. People cannot fulfill that kind of unrealistic demand from another person. Today, one of the top keyword's friends have repeatedly used in describing me with others is independent. This is mentioned because it's dramatically opposing to what I once was in the earlier years. As you evolve your consciousness and all aspects of you, then you are also evolving out of co-dependency and into independence.

It's pretty common to seek out attention and love from external sources from the teenage years on up into one's early twenties. One hopes that by the time you begin moving into your later twenties, your desire for external sources to shower you with love fades and grows less enticing. You realize that the love you crave can be conjured up naturally by standing in your own power.

Exercise does a body good on all levels for this reason. It helps in raising your vibration, energy, and consciousness where you feel alive without the validation of others. You look and feel incredible. It cracks open the psychic line with the Other Side even more. It also helps you heal from illnesses that are healable much quicker.

The last time I was bed ridden with a dramatic flu was 2004. Technically when I was getting sick in those days it was usually from catching it from someone else that was around me. I eventually grew to be so strict that I refused to be around anyone that had a cold or the flu until they were better. It doesn't mean I'm unkind, because if they are someone close to me, I am buying all sorts of healing remedies and a goodie bag that I leave at their door.

This doesn't mean I don't get sick or haven't been sick since, but I just haven't been bed ridden for days or even a day for that matter. I have however felt the initial hints of a potential flu coming onto me. I'm highly aware when something with my body has suddenly shifted. I might have crossed paths with someone that was sick, so I start to feel a bit weak. The second I suspect anything, I immediately always up my game and begin the process of the preventatives, the exercise, the higher intake of vitamin C supplements and foods, and more water than usual.

I also pray to God and call in the healing Archangel Raphael to help prevent what I'm feeling to blow up into more. I believe in both medicinal healing remedies coupled with spiritual healing remedies, then I follow all of this by going to bed earlier than usual. Nine times out of ten I wake up the next morning energized and ready to seize the day. No signs of the illness anymore. It was completely knocked out of the park. This doesn't mean I couldn't suddenly be struck with an illness or that I'm invincible and immune to anything ever happening. It's just illustrating the point of doing the best you can to be hyper aware of your body within and without. When you notice an issue coming on, then do what you can to reverse it if it's a reversible issue.

This is all connected to being in tune to your body, mind, and soul. Be aware of everything happening around and within you every second.

Notice all changes and shifts that take place within you. If it's a challenge coming upon you, then take care of you by taking care of it as fast as possible. Be disciplined about you, yourself, your body, mind and soul. Take it seriously and don't ignore the subtle hints and shifts within and around you, since those can be Divine guidance messages coming in.

CHAPTER FIVE

Expand Your Consciousness

Every soul has varying degrees of psychic abilities regardless if that soul believes in it or not. You are born with a strong degree of psychic clair channels, but somewhere along your human life development, these clair channels become clogged due to negative influences within and around you. The purpose of understanding this is so that you can be aware of what is and what is not dimming your communication with Heaven.

You can be completely clear minded, healthy, and doing all the right things to ensure you have crystal clear communication, but you still feel like you're receiving nothing or that you're being ignored. There is no such thing as Heaven overlooking you. When you feel you're being ignored, then something surrounding you is blocking the communication. When you push to receive a message from Heaven, then the communication is driven further away from you. Pushing for a message shoves it away. The pushing and hoping to make a connection blocks it because there is this anxious, nervous, frustrated, worry energy within. This can be where deep inside you feel you're not going to make that connection. If you're anxious to make a connection with your Spirit team, then this blocks it since it lowers your vibration. A low vibration is the equivalent to cutting off one's oxygen supply to breathe. In this case it is cutting off the oxygen supply to your soul.

Your psychic clair sense channels are telecommunication receptors you use to communicate with your guides, angels, and any in Heaven with. Your various senses are the phone lines to your Spirit team. Everyone was born with sharp senses, which open and close throughout the duration of your life depending on your lifestyle choices, surroundings, thoughts, and feelings. When your clair channels are free of toxic debris, then the clearer the messages and guidance is that comes in.

Your psychic abilities never go away even if it sometimes feels that way. They are under the surface and always accessible. When you don't feel psychic, it just means something is blocking it. Blocks can be certain foods, drinks, negative moods, bad energy, technological distractions, and other people. The closer you are to the physical Earth and nature, then the easier it can be reawakened. This means anything that is not human made.

Some are drawn to the spiritual genre because they're interested in fortune telling. They're fixated on telling the future. Some do not want to know the future, while others are desperate to know the future. You want to know the future when you're in a place in your life that does not make you happy. Your dreams have not been realized. Perhaps you've been single for quite some time and you wonder if you'll ever meet the one.

Much of the time related future predictions are difficult to assess since the mass majority operate on free will choice above Heaven's guidance. This is shifting and altering one's course dramatically every so often. Being more psychic is to also help you make better choices in your life. It's to help ensure that you stay on the right path, which in the end will bring you to your destination of fulfillment on all levels. It's to bring you a healthier and happier existence.

Removing toxins in your life assists in opening up your psychic clair channels wider. There will be negativity that enters your vicinity, but when you're aware of when it happens, then you're able to quickly take steps to modify it and bring you back to that centered space. This is why Heaven advises that you take care of yourself as best as you can. They might guide someone to be alcohol free, since they believe that no one needs any toxic vice if they're governing their life from a place of joy, love, and peace. The high that comes with those traits are beyond what any addiction can satisfy. In the end moderation is important with anything and you're not going to Hell if you enjoy a glass of wine every night, so don't misunderstand this. They're merely explaining that it can block and dim the messages coming in if you're attempting to connect. They feel that toxins are not craved on a regular basis when someone is operating from a high vibration.

In order to be creative you need to have focus, stamina, energy, motivation, and inspiration. When you've been feeling sluggish for days and don't know why, ask your team for help to give you natural energy. You can ask them to guide you to healthy products or to give you the steps you need to take to regain your strength. They may give you a task that is telling you to go to the gym for an hour. After you do that, you leave the gym as if you're floating on air with natural energy.

A successful working Medium friend who assists with solving crime cases informed me privately that she would have one beer or two before she begins filming an episode on television since it relaxes her. She will not have any more than that because then she'll just be all over the place and way too buzzed to connect.

What works for one person will not always work for another. What my Spirit team advises is sometimes a generality. They also reside and operate from a space that is challenging for the ego to get to. They understand the struggles that human beings go through, but they feel that if everyone on the planet operated from the space they do, then there would be peace on Earth and toxic addictions wouldn't be desired. Everyone would be happy because no one is treating others disrespectfully or clawing their way to achieve or dominate. If everyone paid attention to Heaven, then love would reign. Unfortunately, this is not the world that exists today, and human beings are to blame for that design.

You have the ultimate say on what works for you. This is your life and you must live it for you and do what you feel is best. When someone that loves to cook becomes accustomed to how to follow a new cooking recipe, then they may start to alter it a bit and add things here and take away things there. My team relays a structure for you to jump off of. When they make recommendations to watch what you ingest from unhealthy foods, to drugs, to alcohol, then it is for various reasons that include helping you be a stronger conduit with Heaven which simultaneously moves your life into a happier content place.

When you focus on a health issue, then you give more energy and power to it. This expands and makes it worse, which is what you want to avoid. There will be health issues you might be faced with. Your soul is separate from what's happening to your physical body. Avoid labeling and identifying with a health issue. Know that everything will work out in the way that it's intended to. In the end, your soul is always intact regardless of what is happening to the physical body you temporarily inhabit.

You Are What You Consume

The FDA *(Food and Drug Administration)* is indirectly responsible for the premature deaths of many human souls due to their abusive power and control on potentially lifesaving products that are considered illegal in some areas. They are deciding what they think should be approved and what you should or should not ingest in your own body. They are human beings and human beings are flawed. It is no one's place to decide how you choose to live your life pending it isn't harming anyone. The government regulating what others should or should not have needs to be equipped with spiritually based people who have a stronger connection and therefore will know what would be good or not.

At the same time there are products such as hair or skincare that is using ingredients that doesn't need to be cleared with the FDA in the USA at this point. There are activists attempting to get a bill passed where this needs to be the case. Therefore, on the flipside, the FDA can have some benefits if they're able to push cosmetic companies to be more transparent about their ingredients, but then let the consumer decide if they want to continue using it.

There is an excess of human made drugs, foods, or drinks that are considered toxic to your body when taken regularly or in large quantities, but these products are ironically considered legal by the FDA, so you can see how it's a bit of a flawed system.

Some see an issue with marijuana, but they have no issue with alcohol, which is responsible for more accidents, deaths, and harm on other people than weed. The only reason some find an issue with marijuana is because they were taught that it's an illegal drug. It's a plant that comes from the ground long before humankind existed. It is only illegal because the human ego made it this way for various reasons. The government made alcohol legal, which ingrained that into the minds of the human condition that it must be better than weed because it's legal. Weed is only illegal in places because humankind chose to make it illegal. Alcohol is far more harmful than weed.

Flawed human beings make decisions for you. Over time there have been products that were once legal before the FDA banned it and vice versa when they later discovered they made an error in judgment. Examine all of the atrocities and destruction created out of the choice's humankind thought to be correct in the past and you get a pretty good observation into how you are controlled.

This isn't advocating that you smoke weed or drink alcohol. This is illustrating the way human souls perceive things around them. Most of it can be connected to the way they were taught. If you started out on Earth alone with no one else telling you what to do, what to eat, what to drink, then it would be interesting to note how you view your surroundings and how you would survive.

I have had others ask me about what the angels think about eating meat. Angels have said that it's no good. I'm not a vegetarian, but I am fairly strict about what I consume to an extent. They went into that when you eat certain meat or anything that was a living soul, then you are eating that life force. The conditions of animals today in the way they turn them into food is horrific. This means you're also eating their trauma. They're showing me crammed cages in abusive environments. They also explained that it's not a sin to eat meat. They mean it's no good for the human's health long term. There are better exceptions such as if someone is eating meat that is organic, or where the animals are raised for food in loving conditions. There are certified organic farmland where no added growth hormones, pesticides, or antibiotics are used, which is certainly better than the other kinds of meat if you love meat. Things are slowly changing since you can find organic products in the stores now. The animals, plants, sea life, and all of that were partly put on Earth for human's survival. Humankind cannot survive necessarily by eating the leaf off a tree.

No one knows how an animal they're eating was raised. You're not going to Hell if you crave and eat a hot dog at a Carnival. Nor is someone who is a carnivorous eater their entire life going to be sent to Hell and damnation. Like anything that could potentially be toxic, meat should be consumed in moderation and caution should be adhered to with whatever you are ingesting. Ultimately, you make the life choices that feel right to you. Besides regardless of what is said here, your Doctor will tell you what to cut back on if they're detecting a potential health issue down the line due to what you're consuming.

There are many souls sent here to battle the food corporations to get them to make their products naturally or organically. They are also fighting to get food companies to reveal what the product is made of on the label. It is interesting that some of the food companies are fighting right back to avoid having to do that. If what you're using is good, then you'll be proud to show that to the world on a label.

There are organizations that use genetically engineered or modified seeds in their crops. This is otherwise known as GMO or Genetically Modified Organism. When human tampering starts genetically altering anything with chemicals, then you can guess what negative cons will come out of that.

One of the many issues that came out of that was the genetically modified soybean. It first came to light in the early 1990's. The soybean was said to be toxic to human health especially in Men. It drops their testosterone levels and raises estrogen levels at an earlier age than is typical. Estrogen is great in high amounts in the female body, but not the male composition. Examine the male species post 1995 and how they differ in comparison to those of pre-early 1990's. The bottom line is some of the food companies use chemicals that have a high level of toxicity when consumed. Most people are consuming it and not aware of the buildup happening in their body over time.

Food corporations make many products with all of these additives that are bad for you and create toxic build up in your system. This food didn't exist centuries ago and humankind thrived and survived just fine.

The food companies and corporations often make products with all sorts of dangerous additives and ingredients that no one can pronounce or say. You'll note the obvious red flag when you see a long list of ingredients on the package with names you've never heard of or can barely pronounce. These products become addictive because they artificially alter that person's state of mind or mood temporarily into a feeling of joy. The human being has been unable to replicate the kind of euphoric high they felt when back home in Heaven. It is challenging for them to get back to that state when they were a soul before they entered a human body. Therefore, they consume human made products to get there. They become attracted to other addictions to fulfill a hole of loneliness, boredom, depression, or any other emotional state. This is what emotional eating is.

Falling into Addictions

Most of the world's most successful people are goal oriented. They take action and go after what they want even when others tell them they have no business doing something. They pay no mind and continue to work at achieving their goals one after the other. You rarely hear about them succumbing to an addiction such as drugs, alcohol, or bad food. The ones that do fall into the realm of toxic addictions then start to see aspects of their life crumbling. The only addiction the rest of them might be guilty of is one of winning and accomplishing. They're too busy to fall into a depression or time waster. When you're doing work that gives you pleasure, then this raises your vibration. The vibration rises above depression and toxic addictions. You no longer crave those substances because you're high on life.

While disciplined individuals can reach this heavenly euphoric state naturally through spiritual practices, it is still a struggle for human souls to achieve overall in the practical Earth world. The rebuttal or a non-believer might say something like, "You take care of yourself and live nine more miserable years longer than I do. Big deal."

It is a myth to assume that someone who is regimented and takes care of oneself is unhappy. Someone that falls into the bell jar consuming an excess of human made addictions can be an unhappy camper, which is why they resort to toxins to give that artificial lift. Someone on cloud nine and feeling a natural love from within rarely craves a toxic addiction. I know what this is like since I've resided in both ends of the spectrum bouncing back and forth experiencing all of it.

We know I had a drug and alcohol addiction in my early twenties. After I was clean, I was involved in a love relationship in the past with someone who had an alcohol addiction, but craved the alcohol less while with me due to the natural feelings of love that were growing within while around me. When our connection dissolved, you can accurately guess that the craving for high amounts of alcohol rose up once again for this person.

When you're in a healthy long-term relationship, then that reduces or zaps away the desire to consume negative toxins and addictions in high quantities. The reason is love raises your vibration. When your vibration is high, then you don't crave or desire toxins. You are also less addicted to those substances. If you're someone battling addictions to something, then it is often likely you'll fall back into that path while in this healthy loving long-term relationship. This is because the love relationship can only sustain for so long before it is no longer in the newness category. An addicted person may grow bored or start to feel inadequate while in the love connection. They soon reach for the addiction in hopes it will remove those negative feelings. For some they may fall into that addictive behavior, but they're absolved in it far less than when they're single and unhappy.

You are not being criticized if you have an addiction to particular toxic substances and obsessions. As mentioned, I'm a lifelong addict and know firsthand what it's like to have an addiction to alcohol, drugs, vices, cigarettes, and sex. You name it and I probably became obsessed with it. Ironically food was the only substance I've never had an addiction for. With the assistance of my Spirit team over the course of my life I diminished the harder addictions while in my twenties. I became more of a disciplined bloke who worked day in and day out to make it through without succumbing to the addiction as best I could. I've fallen into the addictive behavior from time to time, but hopped out just as quickly, whereas in my twenties I climbed in and stayed in. I'm what some might call a dry addict. This is someone who is not using addictions, but still behaving like an addict. Moderation or elimination is the better alternative in avoiding the dangers of toxic addictions.

Addictions break apart positive connections with others. It has a negative effect on your life path trajectory. They bring on an array of diseases and even premature death. This is enough to scare some out of the addiction. In large quantities, the toxic addictions block and dim the connection with your Spirit team on the Other Side. This isn't in judgment again to those that are battling a serious toxic addiction and who are in and out of treatment. I've been in the trenches of toxic addiction in the past with the drug and alcohol addictions where I've also fell into the bell jar and off the wagon more times than I can count. I understand what it's like to battle addictions having gone through it myself. I also understand the fight it takes to get out of it successfully.

When you're in tune and connected to what's beyond, then your life begins to improve. When you're in tune to the guidance filtering through you from your Spirit team, then you make fewer mistakes. You pick up on the Divine guidance that might be guiding you to your dream job, or to a loving soul mate partnership, to the right car, home, roads to take, and so forth. Being in tune elevates your life in a brighter way. It raises your vibration, which is the space where you are experiencing feelings of love, joy, and peace naturally.

CHAPTER SIX

Detoxify Your Soul

How do you generally feel when you head off to bed every night? How is this feeling carried throughout the next day? What is the energy of the words that pass through your mind as that happens? Is it joyful, stressful, positive, negative, or full of sadness? What is your life like? Do you wake up in the morning and wonder what the point of getting up is? Or do you wake up and feel awesome ready to jump into the day with excitement? How long does that feeling last before you reach for something to give you a lift? What or who causes the feelings to drop? What can you do to change that? What about your thoughts? Are you generally a happy optimistic person or a down feeling kind of soul?

Many factors in your life will dictate the state of mind you will be in every day. If you're someone that desires a loving partnership and it has been years since that's happened, then you will move about each day with some despondence. Even when convinced you're enjoying life and you love your job, but then you head home and realize that you're single and there isn't anyone there to share your life with when you arrive. Maybe you live with a family member or you have a roommate. Those you live with can be a temporary distraction until you realize that ten years have passed, and you don't have a lover.

Perhaps you despise your job, but you're afraid to leave. You worry that you won't find another job and you have bills to pay. Human physical desires convert into toxins that buildup within your soul and this subsequently affects your physical body. It can leave you feeling consistently rundown. This is why it's beneficial to detoxify and cleanse your body and soul as often as you can.

If you're a busy professional always working, then this is especially important. These toxins can also build up if you're unemployed or if you're someone who lounges around the house all day bored with nothing around that excites you. The boredom feeling is what contributes to soul toxic build up. The fear energy of how bills will be paid when you're unemployed or if you will find another job can build up too.

I've had others approach me protesting that they've been drinking non-stop for days and need to stop. The great feeling they had when they started is no longer there. It no longer matters how much they drink because it is not helping. It's weighing them down causing them to feel agitated, lethargic, and unmotivated. You have one to two beers and you get a buzz. You start pounding back additional beers into you to the point that you start to feel out of it. The negative health risks also increase if this is a regular habit.

Pay attention to what you put into your body. Utilize self-control if you've been on a killer streak of consuming toxins in high quantities. When one is experiencing negative feelings or you're super sensitive, then you might reach for a toxic vice. This is more than just having a beer or a glass of wine. It's drinking a six pack or an entire bottle of wine regularly. You feel high for about an hour or two, then you start to come down from that and the feeling is much worse than before you had the drinks. You feel lethargic and it messes with your sleep. You wake up the next day feeling even more gross and sluggish. You count down the hours in the day before you can have another drink again just to make it all go away. Days and weeks have gone by and nothing has been accomplished. Not to mention that you've been unhappy throughout the whole process.

The super sensitive of the world are more in tune and connected than they might realize. You have a greater frequency of psychic reception than others do. Make lifestyle adjustments that are more conducive to your sensitivity levels. This is by being cautious with who you connect, communicate, or hang out with. Follow your gut if you're not feeling like going to a social event you've been invited to. Pick and choose which events you go to and what has the greater benefit to your overall well-being.

A positive way to deal with moodiness, sensitivity, or a rise in negative feelings is to dive into a creative project. Negative feelings are a sign that your soul is starving to create and express itself. It's a great way to unleash and release all of that built up negativity.

When a popular artist in entertainment culture experiences a painful relationship break up, then they often channel that pain into writing songs and making another record. Actors find characters to play that might be the opposite of who they are in order to release any repression and emotional toxins. You don't have to necessarily try to be an actor in films or a singer on stage, but you can take an acting class for the fun of it. You can find positive creative outlets to unleash your downward spiral of emotions. With the way technology is accessible today, you can film your own acting pieces or record it into a microphone even if it's just for your eyes and ears only.

There are times where nothing specific happened to contribute to mood decline. It is the result of a physically inherited genetic disposition. Other times something happened in your life that upset your world. The third way is that the mood decline is a result of what you're ingesting, be it food, pills, drugs, alcohol, etc. You could be eating something that you love, but happens to be high in sugar. It lifts you up only to drop you down to the floor an hour or so later. Keep an eye on what you put into your body regularly and test products out to assess what could be triggering a sudden mood drop. Do a daily test by examining and testing out what products you consume that could be the cause of regular lethargy or negative moods. The most obvious causes are alcohol or drugs, but sometimes it's food you wouldn't think to be the cause of. It can be dairy, too much caffeine, red meat, or the supplements you take.

Caring for Your Skin

When I see the human skin, clairvoyantly it appears to be covered with little cell like mouths all over every inch of your body. It breathes in the pollutants in the air, sucks in the energy of other people, and becomes clogged and closed up whenever any form of toxins hit it. Your skin craves the thirst from touch. It inhales the vibrations in its surroundings. Taking care of your skin and your body as much as possible is vital and beneficial. This means checking out the kinds of soaps, shampoos, and lotions you use to ensure they're not damaging. Some use natural essential oils, which are derived from plants. When anything touches your skin, then these cells drink all of that in. Ensure that what you're putting on your skin isn't toxic. My guides have said that if it is toxic, then it is the equivalent to someone drinking bleach.

Touch awakens these mouths over the skin. This can be through a lovers or friends touch or by the hands of a massage therapist. Massage therapist here means anyone who knows how to massage someone else whether it is a friend or lover. I've seen little kids playing around and massaging their parent's shoulders for fun after a long day at work. This is beyond a massage therapist, even though a professional massage therapist is ideal since they know the right points to hit.

The topic of tattoos has been brought up with me as well. Getting tattoos is a personal choice. I'm surrounded by family members, siblings, friends, and ex-lovers all covered in tattoos. I'm no stranger to it and attract those who are big on self-expression into my world. Tattoos are creative attributes that express one's individualism. There are risks involved with tattoos, such as injecting ink into your skin, which can cause an infection due to bad needles, which I'm sure tattoo enthusiasts are already aware of. There is no denying that puncturing the skin is going to have some measure of effect, but it isn't going to kill you. A needle is puncturing into the skin and depositing ink. There are other parts of one's body that is not tattooed that has just enough visible mouths for it to not be a problem. When one chooses to get tattooed, they should take precautions such as making sure the needles are sterilized and the ink being used is only for them and no one else. It should be looked upon that the work area is as clean and hygienic as anything else in your world.

If anything is touching your skin, you want to

make sure it's not toxic. This includes the clothes you wear too. Some fabrics are made in toxic chemicals that touch your skin. Washing it before you wear it might not always help. There are also some laundry detergents that can be filled with toxins and chemicals, which cause you to break out. They can produce an allergic reaction after you put the clothes on after the wash. You'll want to be mindful of the soaps you use to wash your clothes too.

For women, certain underwear can cause an issue such as thongs, which can contribute to a urinary tract infection or vaginal problems. Certain tight underwear might be sexy, but if that's all you're wearing it can harbor bacteria. High heels are damaging to a woman's feet if that's all you mostly wear as well as constricting tight outfits.

For men, wear boxers more than underwear briefs. The male testes are outside of the body for a reason. It needs to move freely and not be restricted. There are exceptions at times such as if one is playing sports or being physically active, then it needs to be protected, but if you're sitting down all day, then wear boxers. This is more of a guideline of how often one wears boxers as opposed to constricting underwear. Underwear drops the male sperm count and it can take two to three months to reproduce and increase it. Wear that sexy underwear or those hot outfits, but in moderation to avoid potential issues.

Guilty Pleasures

Pray for assistance and intervention daily to be led to the right products that will not be damaging to your body. The obvious toxic culprits are vices or guilty pleasures like alcohol, drugs, nicotine, sugar, salt, fatty foods, and high amounts of caffeine. No one is going to reprimand you for eating a hamburger, unless it's a Vegetarian activist who sneers whenever you eat meat in front of them. The reason the angels are always preaching about avoiding toxins when possible is for your benefit. They know that consuming toxic products in high quantities will block the communication with them. This also contributes to you missing out on beneficial instructions given to you in order to achieve your desires through action steps.

Toxins are a breeding ground for harder health issues down the line. These products also dictate how you will feel. There will be an initial high the toxin gives you, but then it is soon reversed shooting you to the floor. It weighs you down and makes you sluggish, depressed, irritable, and so forth. Who wants to feel that way day in and day out? You reach for the toxin again to get that temporary high. Multiply that every day and visualize what that could possibly be doing to your insides and your aura. You might not think so or care at age twenty-three, but come sixty-three you'll be wishing you had done things a little differently in your life.

Toxins in life are regularly abused more than the good stuff. These are also toxins that the angels feel that no one needs if you structure your life in a way where those cravings are limited or not desired.

Can you blame the world though? Look at the kind of lives that human souls have created. It's been designed in a way that ensures people run themselves into the ground leaving them permanently exhausted, stressed, and dejected. It's a struggle for most to achieve profound happiness, so they reach for toxins in high quantities to help get through it.

You have some form of caffeine to get yourself going in the morning and you keep this momentum every few hours just to get through the day. When you're unhappy, then this drains your life force energy leaving you feeling as if you need high doses of caffeine to feel energized. I've worked with executives in the past who drink soda all day long to keep them flying. This isn't one soda, but many throughout the day. Multiply doing that by two decades and imagine what will happen to you. No matter how much caffeine you have, you're still feeling the constant daily crash. If you overdo caffeine, then this can cause more stress and anxiety within you, not to mention the damage it does to your heart and health over time.

There was a case of a man who abused caffeine to the point where he was diagnosed with liver cancer. Granted before he passed away, he admitted to drinking six to seven energy drinks a day and had a poor diet of pizza and burgers. This is far more excessive than the daily caffeine jolt. He passed away at the young age of thirty-nine.

If you're unable to quit a toxin right away or do

not want to, work on reducing it so that you're indulging it in moderation. Moderation is having an alcoholic drink or a cup of coffee once a day, rather than drinking it until you drop. It's what it's doing to you or will do to you down the line if you're consuming large quantities of it daily. Reducing your toxin intake and balancing it with healthy stuff is a great step in the right direction to being happier, healthier, and more connected with the Other Side.

Let's say that you're unable to quit having a couple cups of coffee to get going in the morning, but you know you want to. Adopt a balance with some carrot juice, herbal teas, or tons of water preceding that as your day continues on.

Incorporate a detoxifying cleanse every so often. This can be where one day you shut off all technological distractions or time wasters. If that's impossible or difficult, then start small where it's shut off for several hours or your personal cell phone is off during your entire workday. Use your sound judgment on when it's practical to do so. You do not want to vanish for days on end when there is an emergency, crises or even death in your life and no one can find you. The technological detox can include spending this day away from stressful and drama filled people. Consume high vibration food into your system such as fruits and vegetables. Notice how you feel when you do this and compare it to those days where you're taking a pound of sugar in your coffee.

More people lead sedentary lives than ever before. You're either parked all day on your rear at an office job, standing behind a register, or plopped in a chair at home with little to no movement for hours on end. Over time this begins to increase the risks of health-related issues, not to mention your energy levels drop and your body begins to feel as if it's eternally out of whack.

Incorporate regular exercise at least once a day if possible. Take frequent walks, jog, or bike when you're able to. If you're suffering from a physical issue that makes exercise difficult, then add in certain exercises that are safe to keep the blood flow moving. When unsure of what you can handle or what is good for you, then talk to a medical or professional licensed expert when incorporating health, fitness, and nutrition related action steps into your life.

Regular exercise is one of the bigger guidance and messages I've received and have been preaching about longer than anything else. Treating the temporary vessel you're renting with the utmost compassion and care is always urged. If you poured something other than gasoline into your car, then it would tear your car up. Treat your body the way you would a car to ensure optimum performance.

Archangel Raphael is the healing angel to call on for assistance with all health and well-being related issues. Ask Raphael or your Spirit team to help in reducing your cravings for toxic vices or to eliminate it knowing deep down that you're ready. Your Spirit team will work with you on that after you have made a specific request to begin the process of reducing or eliminating something you're trying to control. Request to be guided to healthier alternatives and to incorporate a more balanced intake.

Fresh Air and Water

Fresh air is another top important element to awaken your psychic gifts. This is because spirit power is heavy outdoors. The messages from Heaven travel through the molecules of oxygen. Get out there in nature, amongst the trees, grass, flowers, sunshine, and take deep healthy breaths in. Open your windows at home daily allowing the fresh oxygenated air to flow in clearing out all of the toxins that build up in a home with the windows permanently shut. Fresh air means clean air and not smog polluted air.

Many human souls get up every morning five days a week to sit in an enclosed car to go to an enclosed office to sit in all day. They hardly go outside for their breaks. At the end of the day they climb back into their enclosed car to go to their enclosed home, and then repeat the next day. Many cities have built shopping malls, theater complexes, promenades, apartment complexes, and grocery stores on top of one another. It's grown to become void of quiet nature settings. Land developers don't care about trees. They care about building, which isn't a problem until you're building shamelessly and unwisely on top of one another.

Take steps to include more fresh air in your life. Make a pact to take breaks throughout the day where you can get outside and at least walk around the block. When you arrive back home, open all of your windows, and allow the fresh air to waft in if even for a few minutes. Go for walks after dinner, or get in a workout before dinner. Get plenty of exercise and fresh air. These are additional key secrets to integrate into your life in order to awaken the creative part of you, raise your vibration and consciousness, give you a clearer psychic line, and improve all aspects of your body, mind, and soul.

Water governs so much of this planet from the ocean, to the lakes, to the human body. Water is one of the most awesome detoxifiers. This includes bathing, swimming, or sitting in front of an ocean or lake if you're near one. If you're not, then the power of visualization can take you there. Open up ocean photographs on your computer or thumb through a photography book of beaches and meditate on them. Drink plenty of water every day to flush out the toxins in your body.

The world's oceans are critical to human survival and its habitat. It must be kept clean of toxins the same way you keep your physical body clear of toxins. The ocean is what contributes to the clouds that form in the sky, which produces the water your body needs in order to endure life in a healthier way. When one heads to a non-crowded beach, they have reported to feeling more relaxed and alive than they did before they went to the beach. Those that live along the coast have been reported to have stronger health than others might. The ocean breeze blows away smog particles that the rest of a big city would breathe in. It increases your body's ability to absorb oxygen. If you're not near an ocean, or lake, then the water comes to you by drinking it, taking a shower, bath, or through the power of visualization. The mind is a powerful device and can take you anywhere you want to go and bring you anything you desire including what you do not desire, so use it wisely.

CHAPTER SEVEN

*Soul Cleansing
to Motivation*

Many sensitive's shy away or keep away from other people due to the negativity that they often associate with other people. It may not be that every person is bathed in negative energy, but a highly sensitive person is more prone to absorbing every shred of energy from all that it crosses path with that it can become unbearable. Some might call them anti-social or shy, which is the not thought out point of view because it goes much deeper than that. Not everyone is bouncing off the walls in extroverted spirits. Every person on the planet has a built-in composite of personality traits that they're born with, such as the genetic to the astrological, or it's molded into them by the events during their childhood. The highly sensitive person ends up seeing all people as risky to be near, even though there are good and bad energies within every person that exists. Because they sense every nuance, they absorb these energies that people emanate off of them more than other souls do.

There are good people threaded in the mix of the negative, but because both energies are so potent, the highly sensitive person is overwhelmed by the massive energies that dart towards them that it leaves them temporarily drained. Going to crowded places like a mall, amusement park, or grocery store can wear them out. This is why they have to run their life like a strict disciplined executive ensuring their soul and sensitive nature are protected. They learn to be careful about the decisions they make each day that could have an effect on their well-being. This is one of the pluses of being a highly sensitive person. It's that you're more likely to have a keen clairsentient clear feeling psychic channel where you can detect what to stay away from. While another person that isn't as in tune will dive right into danger oblivious of the consequences.

Detoxing your world when it comes to people means being mindful of who you allow into your auric circle. Keep those you see as antagonistic away from you or in small doses if you have no choice. Those you have no choice but to see might be family members or work colleagues. Surround yourself with optimistic positive people whenever possible.

When two positive optimistic go-getters join forces, then there is no telling how far you can both go. You feel inspired by one another, rather than brought down by them. Some of the personality types that can contribute to lowering your vibration just by being in their vicinity can be a gossip, negative complainer or someone that regularly makes toxic choices. When you're around someone like that every day, then this can unknowingly have an effect on you being a positive abundance attractor.

You may be a naturally positive person and feel you're doing everything possible to attract in good stuff, but find that nothing good comes in. One of the blocks preventing this good stuff from coming in can be something you were unaware of such as being around negative people. This will have an effect on what you are attracting into your life.

Being around a Debby Downer will only bring you down and stall you from moving forward. Focus on quality people to surround yourself with such as those that are mutually supportive of you as you are with them. They also allow you the required space you need throughout each day because they understand that you are a sensitive. Highly sensitive people need more time outs alone than others.

Eliminating toxic friendships also includes those on your social media page. The world is drama ridden and chaotic enough with all the daily gossip noise from politically hyped chatter to celebrity gossip. You've likely noticed whenever the latest scandal rises that every other person will post nonconstructive words that come out in a negative toxic scream, whine, or complaint about the target. This does nothing to help anyone. It's toxic energy that fans those flames undeserving of attention. It brings you down, it lowers your vibration, it blocks good stuff from coming to you, and it puts a damper on your life. You then carry that out in the world and spread that to whomever you connect with. Those you pass it to then take that energy and spread it around as well. Soon the entire planet has erupted into nonsensical chaos that helps no one at all.

This isn't just practical advice from Spirit, but those sensitive and more in-tune than others have all vocally expressed having noticed this on their own. They know how it ultimately makes them feel, which isn't a positive uplifting feeling.

I've watched past acquaintances and friends on social media announce that their wall thread is too plagued with negative energy that they plan to take a break from social media. That's one of the great ways to detox from technology for a bit, but at the same time you shouldn't have to run and hide from your own page. Instead you can hide that toxic person's posts or remove them altogether. Some have gone as far as to deleting their account, which might seem extreme. There are ways around that if you want to stay on social media. This is by being exceptionally careful about the types of people you're allowing on your friend list.

One of the positive tools available on some social media sites now is you can unfriend people if you choose to, or unfollow them if you don't want to unfriend them. This way you can keep them in your friends list, but you no longer see their posts. This is beneficial for someone you like, but you can't stand the constant negative posts they keep putting up. I did this myself with people that continuously posted negative posts on the politicians and celebrities they hate everyday all day long.

Popular social media sites at this point are Facebook, Instagram, and Twitter. All three now have this 'hide' feature. Many social media sites are aware this is a problem, so the fact that my Spirit team and I are discussing it is nothing new. If at the time you're reading this, none of those social media sites are around, then there is likely something similar available that can apply to this.

It's rare for someone to post about the positives they like about someone. It's easier for the ego to gossip about who they hate. When someone is unhappy or unaligned, then they are more apt to posting negativity. Happy centered people aren't attracted to negativity and prefer to post constructive positive content.

By the time I was done hiding the repeat offenders on social media, I had a nice clean uplifting page with people that posted more engaging interesting content that was on the positive side. Letting go of negativity allows room for positivity. Positivity brings more positivity.

When detoxing from people and social media, you also want to detox from distractions and time wasters. These are distractions that eat up good chunks of your day from wasteful internet and social media surfing to ,chatting with random people on dating apps that you don't care all that much about. This is knowing that you have work to do or that you could be doing. It's not a crime to have a guilty pleasure you enjoy breaking away to for some fun, such as random internet surfing to chatting with others on a dating app. Chatting out of boredom daily rather than chatting with someone you genuinely have an interest in knowing can lead to more procrastination, non-productivity and laziness.

Clear the Clutter

Clearing the clutter is part of organizing your life. It's included as part of the detoxing process. Detoxing all aspects of your world prepares you to open the gates to abundance and blessings. The clutter clearing is beneficial since it cleans the energy and allows you to focus more clearly. Clear focus equates to a stronger communication connection with your Spirit team. As a writer, I will incorporate procrastination techniques where I need to make sure my space is completely clear of clutter before I fall into the zone to write.

When you walk into a messy room you immediately sense the chaos, which makes your thinking more chaotic and unsettled. Clear away the cobwebs and the clutter by boxing up or throwing away items you will never need or look at again. If it has deep sentimental value or attachment and you're not ready to part with it, then box it up and put it in a closet or storage if it doesn't need to be lying around.

Commit to simplicity and keep your surroundings organized and uncluttered. Extricate friendships that you don't consider to be true authentic friendships, but connections you keep around due to a fear of loneliness. If the friendship stresses you out, then it's time to begin distancing yourself from them. Friendships that are true and long lasting will place no demands on you or your time. They understand this and form naturally unfettered.

This all has an effect on the energy you're creating in your life. If your life has some unseen negative dents in it, then this can create a block to attracting in good stuff.

Detoxing your inner and outer worlds isn't just about detoxing your body of toxic addictions, bad foods, drugs, or alcohol. It's more than going on a fast or cleanse. It's also about detoxing every aspect of your life from clearing the clutter in your home and work life to detoxing the people around you. Do a thorough examination of the people in your world from family to friendships. Who brings you down whenever they come around? Work on eliminating and dissolving those in your life that do nothing, but bring drama and chaos to your world. Even if you don't extricate them, eventually the angels will remove people from your life that have fulfilled their purpose or contribute nothing of positive benefit, but stall you from moving forward. You don't have to wipe out best friendships or family members that you love on some level, but you keep contact with them in small doses. Generally, when someone isn't a fan of a family member, they're usually not spending every mind-numbing minute with them anyway, unless they live with them.

Get structured in your life and plan, schedule, and organize your surroundings. When you have a clear space, you have a clear mind. A clear mind helps you get focused while allowing your Spirit team's wisdom, messages, and guidance to come flowing in. This guidance helps bring you one step closer to achieving what you desire.

Be mindful of the daily or weekly purchases you make. There is a fine line between overspending on things you don't need to buying the occasional gadget or item you would love to have. Buying something for you is part of self-care. It's when it moves into constant frivolous financial spending to fill an emotional void that you begin to block the flow of abundance. You may already know when you're spend-happy to make you feel better. When it becomes a regular habit, then it moves into toxic territory that can have an effect on what you're bringing into your life. Every atom, cell, and matter that exists is energy, regardless if it's physical material items or part of your feelings and thoughts. Breathe new life into all of the energy cells in your world to becoming a clear vessel of reception with God. All wonderful things end up coming out of that.

Get Motivated to Succeed

You might have other distractions such as work or family obligations that seem to eat up your time each day. This is to the point that you have zero time to devote towards your life purpose, passions, or in building your side business. That side business is the one that will eventually free you from the confinement restrictions of being unemployed or from working day jobs you despise. Daily procrastination techniques and distractions can eventually make you notice that a week has gone by where you've donated zero time towards your purpose. Sometimes your ego will have you push that away when realistically you could squeeze in a half hour to an hour each day that consists of one action step towards your passion and purpose.

In the past, I've made excuses that there isn't any time. After weeks of that I started to pay more attention to the downtime I did have. I'd say, "I have forty-five minutes with nothing to do before I need to leave for my dinner. I can squeeze in something important now."

All souls on the planet are worthy and deserving of blessings as any other. When you get into a position where you feel blessed for the good you have now, then this lifts your energy vibration to welcome in more. It also allows you to do good stuff for others when you are no longer filled with other practical day-to-day worries. Once you're taken care of, then it's easier to freely focus on others who could use your helping hand.

Everyone is born with special gifts in the areas

of psychic abilities to creative skills. There isn't one person on the planet that doesn't have something extraordinary about them to utilize and contribute towards the betterment of humanity. At the same time, many distinctly amazing people struggle in low vibrational jobs to physically survive that they end up pushing their authentic talents down to continue on. The angels want to guide them out of that and can help maneuver circumstances to produce blessings to propel that soul forward. It can take them years to decades to help some people, while it seems others are blessed at an early age. It doesn't mean you're less talented or gifted than someone else.

Each person is a special case with varying reasons as to what the delays or blocks are. This is another reason clearing and detoxing your world is beneficial. It helps you become a stronger conduit with the Divine. When that takes place, then you're able to detect the answers clearly as to what is preventing the positive flow of abundance enlightenment.

Avoid placing a time limit on when good things can or will happen. It doesn't matter how old you are since you are not discriminated against from receiving blessings and miracles at any age. There are numerous factors that have to be considered that come into play as to why there are delays to witnessing a positive flow of abundance. Some of those factors require work on your part.

An older person might feel resentment when they see a twenty-two-year-old popular well-known entertainer purchase a mansion worth three million along the coast with a magnificent view. This doesn't mean this popular star is any more deserving or worthy of excessive material abundance over you. In one sense, it might feel like the luck of the draw, or that the maneuvering your Spirit team has been working on behind the scenes is taking longer than another person. It's super easy to fall into envy and resentment in that instance, especially if you've been working so hard and yet are seeing little to no return in the hard-working investment you've been applying for years. Believe me I as well as Spirit understand, but you don't want to wallow too deeply in that energy indefinitely since that will block what needs to come in.

The other side of that is you don't know the challenges and tough experiences the popular star is faced with behind closed doors. You may say you don't care, but despite their fat bank account, they could be battling with issues far worse than you could imagine. Some find it difficult to sympathize with anyone who doesn't have money issues, but when you do that then you're placing higher value on money. That person with money is human like anyone else and going through personal challenges you're unaware of. What matters to Heaven is what is in your heart and who you are regardless of what's in your bank account.

Heaven is also dealing with people that operate primarily from ego and free will. Your Spirit team could be frequently attempting to get the attention of someone important on Earth that can propel you forward, but that person is not picking up on the guidance. You suffer longer because the person intended to make an important offer to you that can change your life is not following the hunches periodically put in front of them. It can also be you who isn't noticing the guidance coming in or following. All of that can create an immense amount of delays.

Due to human free will choices consistently getting in the way of conclusive progress can create an enormous amount of delays to seeing your hard work not reap much reward. Never give up, never lose faith, and never stop believing. Keep telling yourself the breakthrough will come and it will on the wings of Angels. And so it is.

CHAPTER EIGHT

*Clearing the Chaos
Within and Around Your World*

Balancing all parts of the totality of your soul's self are the endless positive potential possibilities. You open up the universe to the blessings of abundance on all levels from the mind, body, and spirit. This is abundance within the soul consciousness mind, the spiritual awareness, and the most enticing to human beings, which are the physical blessings of abundance. This includes the necessary material comforts such as the home, the great job, plentiful finances, as well as friendships and a love partner. There's nothing ill about desiring physical comforts until it moves into greed territory and that it is all one desires. All other aspects need to be in play. For instance, when one's spiritual soul awareness opens up, then this simultaneously draws in positive experiences of abundance.

One of the steps to preparing you to open the floodgates of abundance and blessings and balance in your life may cause some fuss, but it is a simple task that anyone can do for free, nonetheless. This is cleaning and clearing the clutter in your life both internally and externally. It can be clearing out friendships that only bring you down and make you feel bad about yourself, to cleaning up and organizing your home life. Messy discombobulated surroundings can create a disrupted flow of positive blessings of abundance.

You can get into it by consulting with a Feng Shui expert. If this is too costly or doesn't interest you, then do some free research online to gain some basic tips. The clearing of the clutter doesn't need to be perfect, but you might feel you can get more organized than you might be right now. If you walk into your home and you see the disarray with items piled sky high, then take one section a day at a time to get your home organized, so that it's not overwhelming. Disorganization disrupts the energy flow in and around your life. When we say in and around you, then this includes the mind, body, and soul aspects.

Be mindful of the kind of people you hang around with as they can affect your aura and energetic field as well too. If you're around someone that is a perpetual toxic person, then you will absorb that into your consciousness being and will become one with it. Work on dissolving connections that offer you no positive benefit. You don't have to abruptly cut people out, but if you are looking to reduce your contact with them, or dissolve them out of your life, then work on dissolving people the way you dissolve any toxic vice, which is gradually, safely, and slowly. You are available for them less and less over time.

This isn't about abandoning people in a time of need. This is about the offenders that only use you to harshly rant and complain about something regularly that they have no interest in improving. You make constructive suggestions to help them, which is met with retaliation and resistance. Follow this by keeping your options open to add in brighter friendships with those you feel a stronger connection with that are enjoyable to be around and more aligned with who you are or are becoming.

The other benefits to clearing the clutter within and around you are that it contributes to helping you think more clearly. The flow of energy moves swiftly than if you were living in chaotic disarray. When the energy is moving positively, this brings in positivity. When you live in chaos, then that's what you invite in. After my father passed away, I was stunned to discover how he had been living in such disorder. Nonsense piled sky high covering every inch of space that could be found filled with something. I had always seen it and mentioned it to him over the years, but it was after the death when you're going through stuff with family members to sort out that you truly see the disarray.

Sometimes the clutter can come up in the least likely of places. One of the positives of the Internet is that you can purchase most anything you desire without so much as a thought. You can do that from anywhere, such as from your phone in bed in the middle of the night when you can't sleep. You no longer have to fight the traffic and crowds to get a good parking spot at a store, then spend all of that time browsing the aisles, and standing in line to purchase those items.

It's so rare and infrequent that I physically walk into a store. The majority of everything is delivered to me, including groceries! This isn't out of laziness, since others have explained I'm one of the least lazy people they know. Part of the delivery bit is the convenience, but the other part of it is due to my severe social anxiety and the tampering of chaotic psychic energies absorbed while going to a crowded place filled with disgruntled people like in a retail store.

The downfall to this ease of ordering stuff online is that there are now numerous statistics popping up all over the place indicating a dreadful vision. The world in general is hoarding more products they don't need due to impulsive online shopping. There was a point I had walked into my place and noticed all of these items sitting around in boxes that were delivered. My heart sunk in a feeling of devastation. I couldn't believe what I had allowed to happen, "What is all this? How do I have all this stuff? For what purpose?"

I decided to give it away to people who could use it. Giving away clothes sent to me by that label that I never wore or took the tags off. Labels and vendors send me stuff on top of that due to the position I'm in. I had become what I thought I would never be.... a hoarder. Luckily, it wasn't a lifetime of collecting, but more like several weeks. This was several weeks too long that I had to get rid of it all. If I've never used it, then I never will. I then looked up local charities and places where people were suffering from material lack and brought it to them.

Most people admit that the stuff they buy they don't really need. They end up throwing it away creating a bigger trash situation. This is a planet of hoarding! It's become another addiction even for those who don't like shopping. They hit, "add to cart", and then click that "buy" button and a chemical rush of Dopamine lifts them up.

Dopamine is that high happy feeling one gets from things like food, drugs, alcohol, sex, shopping, and on and on. It is anything that makes someone feel good.... temporarily. Because once that high drops astronomically, which it will sooner than later, you crash suddenly feeling low again and are out in search of another fix. You race to get that addictive fix like a drug injection that gives you another temporary high to keep going.

Some consume this false happiness where they do this daily just to stay happy and keep going. It never lasts and winds up leaving you craving another fix. When the package you ordered arrives, then that dopamine fix hits you again to open that brand-new package. But what do you do with that package after opening it? I've discovered that some never even take it out of the wrapper. It gets tossed aside to sit on the counter for a week or two until you mumble, "I need to put this away. I never even took this out of the wrapper."

Because of the ease of buying online, you're not paying much attention to how often you add to your cart and click purchase. There are people who are exceptional at watching what they spend. Some don't have the money, or they don't own a credit card, and they're just trying to get by with the basics. For others, myself included, I've had to learn to be extra cautious. I'm usually cautious as it is, but sometimes I'm looking at what's being delivered and wondering, "Did I really need this contraption? What possessed me to buy this?"

It took some additional self-discipline to realize I was being sucked into the new trend of online shopping and hoarding without realizing it. Compared to others it wasn't as bad as I'm not that much of an impulsive shopper. I've never liked shopping unless there was something specific I needed. I wasn't one of those people buying additional pairs of shoes or clothes I knew I would never wear. I'm the opposite extreme where I've worn the same pairs of shoes until they grow torn. That's my cue to buckle down and get a better pair of shoes. I never bought the latest iPhone, but would use the same version for years long past its upgrade eligibility date. I'd keep using it until key features like the home button would stop working. That would be clue that it was time to buckle down and change the phone because the buttons are no longer working.

While some people revel in the latest gadget craze, I saw no difference. Plus, the hassle to transferring everything over to the new device was too much of a chore that was never worth it to me. If the phone still works, then I'm keeping it.

Other things to keep in mind are that manufacturers are using cheaper materials to make items, which means they break or tear sooner than later, so you have to keep buying the same gadget or item repeatedly over the years. I had regular oscillator fans that seemed less powerful in its breeze a year after it was bought. I soon realized I had to keep replacing them the way you change your tires or brakes regularly on your car.

Clothes are also getting holes or shrinking sooner than later after a few washes. You have to replace those regularly. While the trend to be more environmentally safe or conscious has risen, that hasn't necessarily shown when it comes to how much material is being dumped into landfills. According to many statistics, that number has increased astronomically, which means the environmental craze hasn't improved much.

Many Universities and Colleges have reported enormous shocking statistics surrounding how much waste students collect or are unused. Tons of waste is discarded or donated if the student hasn't bothered to do it after vacating their dorms. The waste that the planet tosses on a large basis can make anyone with a heart, soul, or conscious break down. It's an eye opener when you know about this massive waste and that there are people around the world struggling to survive barely able to afford food. The amount of waste that could be donated to organizations that can help people in need is staggering. There is no mobilization, protest, or marching over circumstances like poverty or child abuse.

A great deal of stuff donated to places like the Goodwill aren't getting sold there either. They end up getting dumped in a landfill as well in the end. You order something online because it's easy. You think it's no big deal if the item isn't what you wanted in the end because you can return it. When it comes to returning items bought online, a great deal of people admitted they don't bother, because it takes a bit more effort to find packaging for it, printing out the proper return slips and receipt, then driving down to the mail carrier service. Most people find it's not worth it to go through all that unless it was a super expensive item.

A messy house, aura, ambiance, surroundings, and life contributes to messy abundance attraction energy. It creates a block due to the restricted flow of your physical surroundings, which simultaneously creates imbalance. If you are a sensitive in tune being, then you no doubt have noticed that when you've walked into a cluttered filled room that you can feel the dark weight of that. When you walk into a space that is free of clutter, then this uplifting feeling rises inside you. Everything in and around you has an effect on your well-being state, including the things you would never consider to have an effect.

Conduct regular space clearing exercises where throughout each year you periodically walk around your house and examine what needs to be boxed up and put away. Look at what needs to be re-organized and set up in a better way. Move furniture around if you have to in order to create a more ideal set up, which can assist in the flow of abundance energy.

When you walk through each room of your house, how do you feel? Are you disappointed at the mess? Do you feel joyful and clear minded? Do you feel a heaviness?

Any negative feeling felt is a clue that some re-organizing needs to be conducted. If you find you're too busy or you keep putting it off, then set a disciplined schedule. This can be where you rely on the seasons changing to re-organize. When it's the first week of Spring, Summer, Fall, and Winter. Use those dates to begin the space clearing if you're someone that procrastinates or keeps putting it off. Light some sage, incense, or candles to help purify the air. Open your windows daily if for at least fifteen minutes to an hour to clear the old air with the new one. I know that can be tougher to do in colder climates, but do what you can and when you can. You know what you can tolerate and get away with without it harming your comfort or health.

When you sage your home, pay attention to corners of your house where energy gets stuck. As someone with Clairvoyance, I've seen darkness in corners of homes and buildings, which show up as floods of insects. There is trapped dark energy in corners more than in any other spot. Have the intention of ridding it as you sage and clear your space. Also pay attention to doorways, which can be entryways for toxic dark spirits.

Clear your aura and spirit, which you can do with sage smoke around your body as well too. You can take a cleansing shower or bath with Epsom salts and essential oils, or you can simply have the intention of clearing your aura by calling in Archangel Michael, Archangel Raphael, or Archangel Jophiel to clear you and your space of any toxic negative energy in all directions of time.

Part of cleansing you, your space and home with sage is also paying especially important care to your bed area. You most likely spend a great deal of time in bed. It's important to clear that energy regularly. If you go to bed in any negative state or if the night is met with tossing and turning, negative feelings, thoughts, or bad dreams, then ensure you clear the bed with sage or whatever tools you prefer to purify it as a precaution.

Sometimes all you need to do is sit or stand in silence and prayer, eyes closed, and mentally call in God, your Spirit team, and only those beings of the highest vibrational nature. You can say something like: *"Please clear me now of all negative toxic energy I've absorbed or created in all directions of time. And so it is."*

You might choose to create an altar or sacred space in your home used primarily for prayer or to help you get more spiritually focus. Burn candles and diffuse nice smells with essential oils to incense, sage, or cedar burning. Candles are great to help give you a focal point. The light of a candle is also welcoming for angels who enjoy the light that is not harsh or tampered with such as artificial or florescent light.

Be careful with your tech gadgets and how they're situated near your bed. There are also growing scientific statistics showing the negative effects on you and your well-being when tech gadgets are so close to you while sleeping. It's more likely than not most people tend to have their cell phones near them all the time. They've become extensions of us. Imagine what that's like and the repercussions that can come out of that. A great many people also live in smaller places or apartments where it's not realistic to hide where their computer equipment is situated. You can consider it covering it when it's not in use. You do the best you can with how you're setting it up, so that it's not affecting your well-being and sleep.

CHAPTER NINE

*Gossip Machine
to Centered Light*

Looking down on Earth it's deathly quiet from the vantage point of space, except for the subtle sounds of electromagnetic vibrations moving through the Universe. Circumstances on Earth appear trivial from that perspective. It's a similar view from Heaven as spirit beings take note of the low vibrational noise and bickering energy coming out of the billions of Earthly souls that put up endless resistance refusing to come together in peace. They want to see someone that is kind and compassionate, but shares a different viewpoint than you, and yet you still accept them for their differences. This is what brings about a Utopian paradise more than anything else. It's that one small step towards active compassion.

Spots of rose light mixed with tinges of white and gold are sprinkled around the planet in the higher vibrational souls that move about attempting to counteract and temper those that run their life from the darkness of ego, but the ratio to the darker souls is on the minimal side.

Part of creating more balance in your world requires talking about areas that are not considered joyful topics. When one considers improving your well-being in the spiritual genre it tends to stick to the airy-fairy light and sunshine bits, while ignoring the root of the issues that reside in the Darkness. Gossiping is one of the majority of these issues that human beings live their daily lives in unable to break free from.

The act of gossiping is one of the dominate forms of expression on Earth, but it has a damaging vibration energy surrounding it that feeds the Darkness. Gossiping induces a temporary joyful rushed high before you experience the inevitable hard crash leaving you wanting more of that fix. Certain personalities and dispositions become extremely addicted to it over others. The effects are similar to that of a drug, alcohol drink, or sugar high. The gossip is either unaware of its toxic effects or they don't care, which would then make them a sociopath void of empathetic emotions.

Gossiping is a lower vibration energy that does nothing to positively benefit anyone. The lower self and ego receive a quick high from gossiping that deludes them into thinking they have a superior voice. Someone with high self-esteem has no desire to gossip, because they are sure of themselves. When you are sure of yourself, you're not looking to engage in gossip, which is designed to cut others down to make you feel better.

High self-esteem people desire good vibrations in their life and will automatically throw up a wall around them when negativity or gossip is in their vicinity. Those drawn to gossip do so out of boredom. They're addicted to the high, because they're experiencing and battling with some form of misery inside. It makes them feel good to attack, lash out, or negatively gossip about others. Productive focused people are not drawn to gossip and are too busy to entertain it. Happy people live in joy and surround themselves with others that are optimistic, pleasant, and positive. They know gossip brings the energy down. You've likely witnessed this when you or someone else is in the line of fire of a negative complainer. You try to wiggle out of there and brush it off to get away from them. You can feel your joy filled serenity being tarnished and dragged down.

The same way there is a dark and light ego, there are also varying levels of gossip from the harmless to the dangerous. The harmless gossip would be you expressing concern for a friend you suspect is going through something tough they won't tell you about. A mutual friend informs you in confidence that this is taking place. This kind of gossip is to get to the bottom of what's happening with a friend with the goal and intention to help them. The dangerous kind of gossip is the lies or negativity that others spread about someone. "Loose lips may sink ships" was a popular phrase coined around World War II that ended up being about the dangers of gossip and how detrimental it can become.

Gossip is dangerous to your health whether you are the negative gossiper, or you are within the vicinity of a gossip. As an innocent bystander to gossip you will absorb that energy into your aura becoming one with it without intending to. This lowers your vibration and brings your energy down while blocking Divine guidance in the process. Eventually the gossip rush causes you to crash to the ground, thus driving you out in search of that quick fix again. The health dangers of gossip are destructive and damaging. Negative energy of any kind will affect your overall health and well-being in the long run. The same kind of rush that the ego receives over gossip is what drives one to obsess over the latest media stories propelling them to post about it on their personal social media accounts.

Common keywords in a media headline used to entice the ego are words such as, "Outraged, blasts, blasted, slams, slammed, under fire, uproar, offends."

Gossip columnists and bloggers use low vibrational turmoil-ridden words to entice someone's ego and lure you into the drama! Notice how adding an exclamation point to the end of that sentence altered it into something uncomfortably dramatic. It gives you a rush of anxiety, nervousness, or adrenaline luring you into its web to pay attention. This is a goal that it gravely succeeds at. It can stop achieving this result when the masses wake up their consciousness and avoid giving it attention. Unfortunately, there are millions of souls threaded around the planet that reside right in the epicenter of that darkness. They're drawn to it on a daily and regular basis. Log onto any social media site and scroll to witness the endless gossip being darted out into the universe.

A realist falls between the optimist and a pessimist. The realist doesn't wear rose colored glasses and nor do they see things through a hazy filter. They see things as they realistically are. Being optimistic is a positive virtue and not necessarily a bad one, pending that the optimist considers all of the data that things might not go according to the way they want them to go in the end.

Life is brighter when you're in a positive optimistic mindset, which is certainly better than the mindset of: "We're all doomed!" Because that's not technically true. One could easily say the human race has always been doomed, but it's the human race that put itself in that position. If the end of the world were to happen, there's nothing you can do about it anyway, so let that go. Typing it out in a seventy something character bite on social media will not stop it.

The way to accelerate life on Earth towards Utopia is if every person on the planet resided in their soul's true nature, which is in a state of all love, joy, and peace. It's virtually impossible for millions of souls to exude that state around the clock in today's ego driven physical designed modern world governed by the darkness of ego. It is counterproductive to their true nature, so people live under constant stress as a result.

When there is discord, then one needs to remain neutral and objective while finding the right balance between opposition. Most extreme issues can be compromised on, which is the quickest way to success. A balanced judge or authority figure stands in the middle hearing everyone's point of view before deciding on the best course of action.

Balance in human lives is lacking and the world is plagued with division between opposing viewpoints not hearing or seeing the other person's point of view. Eventually or hopefully people will figure out that if you can't beat them, then join them. This doesn't necessarily mean agreeing with their stance. If after much discussion both come to some kind of middle ground instead of a rigid unbendable extreme viewpoint, then balanced compromise is reached. People are more likely to be happier and content on all ends when they're not attempting to oppress one side so that the ego can get what it wants with no care about anyone else.

I've conducted studies where I've locked two people in a room together with severely opposing views and values forcing them to connect. By the end of the day, it's not surprising to find that both people walked out of there having gained compassion and respect for the other person, even if they didn't necessarily agree with them. When you have a one on one civil calm discussion with someone with an opposing view, you make further headway than hiding behind the safety net of a mob with pitchforks emotionally ranting and raving about. People don't respond positively to anyone screaming at you, so therefore nothing is improved with aggression.

The mob mentality is predominately on the Internet and social media, which allows people to be louder than they normally would be in person. People band together with their pitchforks to spend a day vilifying someone with constant badgering over something that is generally a minor human crime that people can honestly get over. In the end, they do get over it and completely forget about it in a few days when another story to gossip about is thrust to the top with a bullet.

The mob mentality is associated with the same ones that engage in violent protests, which the world has witnessed all throughout Earth's history and on up into the post technology days. If you examine and study each of those protests to see if what they were protesting about worked in their favor, you will find it to be rare that anything good or positive came about from it post technology. It worked out to change policy by giving women the right to vote or during the civil rights movement, but not post technology. Most that make up a good chunk of the world see it as drama and tantrum energy, neither of which sways the opinions of the recipient or those who agree with the stance. The calm peaceful protests made better headway to successfully helping a cause, because most people respond to calm peaceful advocacy over violent outbursts.

If you genuinely care about an issue or don't like the way something is, then you find a positive action step to implement. Talk to Congress and peacefully explain why the change you wish to see is necessary. Get a job or volunteer in Government to work from the inside out. If it's something you passionately care about, then it could be connected to your life purpose. Destroying people and property over something you dislike is called war where no one wins.

The paradox is that the same people opposing war are the ones creating the destruction of innocent bystanders and property. In the end, what they were protesting about never positively changed anything. It creates a dramatic ruckus and soon evaporates dissolving away having accomplished nothing. The darkness of ego feels more empowered in a group, therefore the idea of roaming the streets in a protest sounds fun and exciting to it. That is until you have to get back to your regular life that entails becoming responsible by getting a job to be able to pay your bills.

Social media has its grand benefits of creating friendships and staying in touch with family, but the dark side of it is that it feeds the mob and the gossip machines. You have to leave it numerous times if you're bombarded with negativity in your thread. When it gets to be insanely bad, then take a breather or a technological detox. You've noticed the out of control gossip and negative ranting's that persists on people's pages. You end up hiding those people who are repeat offenders. They can't see how far they've fallen and are unable to get over whatever it is they are ranting about. It's their page, so they can post what they want, but you don't have to be subjected to it if you're not interested in the daily absorbing of it.

Follow this hiding or removal of repeat offenders by following and liking high vibrational happy pages and accounts, so that it will be what dominates your social media feed for the most part. You may let some negative posts go here and there as everyone has their bad days, but if you see the same person enacting harsh attacking energy on every single post for months on end, then temporarily hide them for a while until they calm down. Check back weeks or even months later, and then scan their wall to see if they're back to the person you once knew before they fell into the darkness of ego disguised through emotional and mental instability.

I've conducted social tests where I've hid repeat offenders, then gone back to their page after months or a year later to see if it was safe to see their posts again. Not surprisingly a year later the original offender was still negatively ranting about the media and politicians, but I also noticed their posts had little interaction on it. It had dropped off over the year because that many people got tired of absorbing the same demoralizing energy over and over. The only person oblivious to the drop off rate was the perpetrating offender lost inside the darkness, except now they were posting to no one. One of the offenders was ironically an angel card reader, which might seem unusual considering that your readings with Spirit are tainted while in the mind space of drama, gossip, and pessimism. After a couple years of that I noticed the angel reader was able to have that awakening moment where they discovered they had been out of control. They admitted the Darkness had got a hold of them, hooked them in, and kept them enslaved in that energy, until finally one day the Light came bursting in lighting his way out of that.

The other negatives perpetuated on the internet that affect the soul are reading fictional media pieces. Many websites contain recycled material that comes off more like a blog than a credible news source. Unless it is a prestige's journalist the rest of the journalists rarely do their research or homework anymore. They just lift the information off of other sites and put it on their own site. You later discover that it wasn't accurate to begin with. It's like someone in school copying another person's paper that also got the answers wrong. Before technology, newspaper editors would refuse to run a story if it wasn't fact checked to a hair-splitting degree as being verifiably true. Many stories were scrapped and not allowed to run if one fact was off. That's not the case today where they run it anyway. I've heard from media site editors that have informed their writers to just run the story regardless of the accuracy of the piece. This is because time is money and they have to keep posting to keep viewers going to the site. It's a business after all and the way to stay in business is to give your audience what you know they'll gobble up regardless of the content.

History has been erased and re-written to the

point that some of it is no longer accurate. The media will take a story and begin altering it and passing it around as if it's fact. What originally happened is no longer part of the story.

It's important to discuss the dangers of the media because it is what dominates and controls the minds of the public. It is typically corrupt, malicious, biased, salacious, and feeding you altered truths that are sometimes manipulated until it isn't true anymore. Humankind has been doing that since the beginning of time. There are endless cases where a story was told in archaic days. Someone else takes that story and begins to alter it, and then another alters that one. Eventually the story becomes more of a fable than a true account of what actually took place. All throughout history this has been the case from the Bible, to the news, to celebrity stories, to school ground gossip. One of the ways the devil works through people is to destroy them through lies. Mentally question what you're reading and if it makes sense instead of following it because your news source of choice hates the same people you do. That doesn't make them accurate.

Remain neutral and balanced since you can't rely on your sources to be. Be the example and stand in the center in the middle hearing all sides, doing your homework, studying up, listening to opposing people objectively and without emotion. Move into the rational thinking part of your consciousness. Seek out media that appears to generally be objective and neutral where it seems the journalist is not taking a side, but merely giving you the facts and the story.

Many spend a good chunk of their time thinking about gossiping or judging others, including well-known people online or in person with anyone that will listen. I've worked in office environments before the author work and that was the top conversation that flies around. It was like that in each one, so it's safe to say that's the general overall way that people live. That's their main topic forms of conversation. Imagine sitting in that dark toxic atmosphere absorbing all of that undesirable energy all day every day. If you're exceptionally sensitive, in tune, and psychic, then you could agree that the energy surrounding them is permanently miserable. They're typically negative about everything beyond that. Now imagine being in that mindset day after day, year after year, and decade after decade until the end of that person's life. The only people that would want to be around someone like that are similar souls, which is why like often attracts like. You bring in the kind of people that match your vibration more or less. Those who are exactly the same would flock to that person.

If you're finding you keep attracting those types in and it bothers you, then take a step back, and adopt a higher view of yourself to see if you are guilty of it too. Sometimes one can easily find they don't like the drama, gossiping, and judging, yet they fall into that pattern when they're around certain friends or colleagues. It's easy for energy to stick to something, so in this case your energy attracts this person to you. You become one with it and then your energy gets stuck in that long after the conversation has ended. It takes work to pry it out of there and take a higher view.

Taking a higher view requires endless hard work that you have to do by the will of your thoughts and actions. The ego is trained to be attracted to the density of triviality and superficiality. It doesn't require much work to be in that space. Raising your vibration and rising above that takes more discipline than people grew up learning to do.

Spend at least a half hour or more without uttering or thinking words that are judgmental. Just 'be' and see what happens. To 'be' means to be still, be focused, and be present. Let go of any negative thoughts. Avoid judging yourself if you find that you're judging. Let it all go as if you're holding a bird in your hands cupped together. Lift your hands upwards and release the bird that takes flight away from you. You're letting go and releasing all of those thoughts, erasing the mental chatter, and the lists. Imagine you're walking through paradise breathing in the amazing fresh air breeze. Breathe in deeply and exhale out pessimism.

Choose to rise above negativity by showing some beautiful poised class. Stay centered in grace and love despite any whirlwind of darkness surrounding you. Nothing is truly as bad as it seems. When a line is crossed, then you graciously intercept it by focusing on solutions rather than creating unnecessary issues. What you focus on will multiply, so you want to make sure it's positive. If you find you fall into the epicenter of negativity, then work on moving past that and in bridging the gap between all souls, including the ones that hold a differing perspective than you.

Look at the positive aspects of a situation or walk away from it. Divert your attention to the blessings in your life, and steer clear of the intoxicating drama and gossip that attempts to lure you into its sticky trap. It does nothing to help anyone and improves nothing, but contributes more hopelessness to the nonsense.

While you're urged to be positive, this doesn't mean living in denial either. You will experience negative thoughts and feelings on occasion. Some will experience it more than others. This isn't about pretending those negative thoughts and feelings don't exist. It's about acknowledging it when it happens, and then take action steps to alter it into something positive and proactive rather than reactive.

Don't feel guilty for being angry that you're stuck in one-hour gridlock traffic driving to a location that is only fifteen minutes away. This is about recognizing when you're feeling that way and looking at ways that work to bring that back down. When someone is in a negative state, then more mistakes are made.

When a driver is angry, they become erratic and reckless. Minutes later in a fury they get into an accident. This is a perfect example of how a negative state can overpower you. This is about being more careful and mindful, but don't feel guilty for feeling negative. Be aware that it's happening and seek out ways to resolve what you're angry about to move past it. Focus on activities that bring you joy and peace rather than negative energy drainers.

To shield yourself from harsh energies, each day call upon the Archangel Michael to blast away negative harmful energy from your aura. Ask him to surround you with protective white light allowing only high vibrational love to enter. You can do this by mentally calling out to him and requesting it in your own way, since there is no right or wrong way. You are heard the second you call out to any heavenly being.

CHAPTER TEN

*Balancing Your
Inner Spirit*

One of the many ways to create more balance in your life is by dissolving toxic people. This is done safely and gradually in the same way you dissolve any toxic vice. Some people will be harder to remove if you feel attached to them or have deeper connections to them such as a family member or friendship that you've outgrown. You can't leave, but you can't stay, and so you're left torn not knowing what to do. Cutting a close connection out abruptly without warning can bother anyone on the receiving end. You eventually reach the point where you say, "I love you, but I love me more."

There are also the toxic people that are impossible to remove at this particular time such as those you work with. In those cases, you won't be able to kick them out of your life, but you can take some disciplined measures to protect yourself. These would be things like calling in the Archangel Michael to shield you with protective white light. That's what you can do spiritually. As for physically, you can keep your distance from them. Keep dialogue to a work related minimum and putting up a cold distant reserve. You're not doing this because you're unkind. You're doing this because you care about you.

You take care of your own well-being first and extract from your life whatever you feel is not jiving with your higher self. This can be whatever is stalling or keeping you from moving forward and upward, but it's not something that anyone can tell you to do. You already know what you need to do and how much you can tolerate before you've officially reached the limit. It's not an easy move to make getting rid of certain toxic people. It's one that you'll do when you feel totally amazing about it and are ready to do.

With toxic friends you once loved, but have found it's become consistently too much, then you can busy your life with other things. Grow more distant from them and be less available. If they complain or cannot handle that you're distant, then that is their issue to wrestle with. What are they going to do, sue you for being distant? This is your life and you are the owner of it.

Moving Out of the Dark Ages

Times have changed where children are handed a technical gadget early on over interpersonal bonding. This sets the stage for relationship suffering when they grow older. This is already seen post 2000 when Earthly life dramatically changed due to the rise in technology and commerce. Technology can be an issue when it dominates preventing anyone from having successful interpersonal relationships. If you use a technological device to post or comment something negative, then you are using the device for harm. It's like handing a psycho a loaded gun. When parents or teachers are dealing with a child that is restless or having a tantrum, they immediately hand it a technological device to keep it quiet so they can be in peace. From an early age, that child sees technology as the way to go.

I grew up in a time before cell phones, internet, and social media, which dates me. There were cell phones, but it was primarily only a small amount of super rich people that owned one and those were the mobile phones that were built into their cars. If you were trying to get a hold of someone, you'd try their home phone, pager, office line, or car phone if they had one. People had a long list of phone numbers in those days. The Internet and computers were coming out, but again that was also primarily used with the rich. There was no social media that gave rise to the darkness of ego and low self-esteem and unhealthy competition. I have the differing perspective of having lived before that time as well as what it was like afterwards. Today one has to watch what they say and how they say it. That's not the world I grew up in. You spoke your mind and people could take it or leave it.

Earth reached high noon on 11/11/2011 *(not 12/21/2012 as some believe)* when the light was equal to the dark. You'll notice how many centuries it took to reach high noon. Before 11/11/2011 is what was called The Dark Ages. After that date we began moving out of the Dark Ages, but it will still continue to be Dark for centuries before those violent dark times are over with. You'll note how many centuries it took to reach this high noon where the Light and Dark were equally balanced. This is about how long it'll take before the Light will be completely dominating. The positive to all this is that we're now going back in the other direction towards the Light. Humanity continues to have a long way to go before global Utopia exists on the planet. As long as love is non-existent in the hearts of the majority, then that is how long it will take to officially be in the heart center of the Light Ages. Having love in your heart means showing love to those who are different from you or who have a differing opinion than yours. What a challenging thing to do!

Humanity is gradually moving in the other direction where the Light is expanding greater than the Dark. It will take centuries ahead to reach that place where the Light dominates and has taken over. We're moving in the right direction, but when it's come to human evolvement it's at a snail pace.

You've likely noticed the tantrums around the world going on in places. They're not pleased with the Light taking over, but this is what is intended. You've got half the world with a consciousness that is rapidly raising, while the other half is settled into the Darkness. It is a war between the Light and Dark, but if there is any truth it is that the Light always wins in the end.

The light workers, warriors of the light, the realm souls, and light warriors, all of them are not exempt from falling into the darkness or into the ego on occasion. Some may be attracted to it more than others. When you're in a weakened state, you fall into the drama of the chaos, the noise, the media, and the politics. It's easy to become enticed by the allure of all that and then become one with it since it's all people talk about in an antagonistic way. To remain centered and balanced it's best to avoid it and not get into the attacks and gossip of it all, because in the end none of that matters. What's intended to happen or take place at this time will be. This is regardless if it's not what someone wants or not. You have to stay focused on what's important. It's understood you want to stay somewhat informed, but those that are attempting to stay informed wind up falling into the allure of the drama. It takes incredible self-discipline to rule your life in a high vibrational state as much as possible.

If you're on the fence wondering if the media and the news is beneficial to you, then try out this exercise. Keep a journal for a month and write down every single thing that bothers you. This means a trending topic you found yourself falling into. After enough time has passed revert back to that journal to see what you wrote down and notice if it has truly had any positive effect on changing your life, or if it was just another time waster you fell emotionally drawn to, but could care less about weeks later. It will be mind boggling to witness the long list of time wasters that prevented you from being happy, moving forward, and acting in life.

Focus on your life purpose rather than time wasters. Look to see if there is something specific in the media that deals with something you passionately care about such as immigration, gay rights, environmental issues, etc. If one of those feels like a stab to the soul whenever you hear it, then this is a sign that it could be connected to your life purpose and mission. If that's the case, then take action steps in doing highly valued research into how you can help surrounding the issues you care about that will create a change in policy. This does not include ranting and raving in attacks on social media.

What you set out to do in the realms of your purpose and life mission is creating change even if you don't feel like it is while in the midst of it. You may think that someone else will take care of an issue, but no one really is or does. If you need to go it alone, then you have to go it alone and tackle it one issue at a time. One small action step can get the energy flowing in that direction. Research and seek out ways where change can be made in the area of your interest that you strongly feel needs to be improved, otherwise let it go.

Stay Focused and Ignore the Noise

One of the purposes for some is learning to ignore harmful words said about or to you. Don't allow it to permeate your soul consciousness. People are going to say negative things at some point around you. It has nothing to do with you, but more to do with what they're battling with internally. If they're saying negative things about you, then they're more than likely doing it to everyone. That's their issue to wrestle with and not yours. You have a higher more important calling, which is to stay focused on your soul's Divine purpose.

Public figures have had to learn to ignore negative words from strangers, since they hear it through public forums more than anyone else. Because they're thrown into the public eye in such a severe way, many of them quickly mastered the art of ignoring it or not paying attention to it. Not all of them follow that mantra and will attack back, but in those cases, they're trying to defend themselves. If someone says something untrue or slanderous about you, then the natural reaction is to correct it. There's nothing ill will about correcting it as long as you remember to try and do it through assertive poise. The top choice is to ignore it and walk away, but that can be hard to do if the words are fictitious and affecting your good name.

Some public figures know to not log online and read stuff posted about them, while others have chosen not to have a social media account. Sometimes they might hear it from those around them personally and professionally, but the ones that master it are careful about who they allow into their private world. They also grow a thick skin in business learning to let certain things roll off. Despite all this they also wrestle with self-doubt like anybody else, but in the end, they ignore it and go after what they intend to regardless. They have a job to do and can't afford to drown in self-doubt that is powerful enough that it is paralyzing them.

When you make mistakes, you correct them, learn from them, and then avoid making them again. That's how you continue to grow and evolve. Everyone makes mistakes as that's part of life, but the crucial element is to learn from the mistakes. Work on avoiding placing blame on yourself or someone else for those mistakes. Mistakes are made to learn from in order to grow and evolve.

Self-Doubts

I've had my share of self-doubts in the past, but that was more so during my teens and twenties than any other age. By the time I turned thirty, I had become Divinely invincible to the point that others around me noticed the massive change that took place with me. I had a master class running big budget films for the movie studios throughout my twenties. The things you are doing now are preparing you for what's next. Whenever I'd start a new film production, I'd have minor doubts that I couldn't do it or that I'd get fired after the first week. After the first week or so those feelings would subside. The thoughts also weren't plaguing me into feeling paralyzed with fear. It was a small thought that might creep in for a second here or there, but then the drive and determination to do the job I was hired to do would overpower any negative thoughts and would quickly dissolve.

I refused to allow negative self-doubt or fear to overpower and cripple me, so the thought might enter and exit super quickly as I adjusted and focused on what I needed to do. When you're going to be one of the coordinators of a film production for a studio worth over $100 million dollars with a crew that will exceed 600 people, then some measure of adjusting to get into it is typical.

The night before every film production job would start, I would meditate for hours and move into the space of the role that I chose to take on. I would show up the first day on the job and immediately take over and fearlessly dominate my role. Any fear that might have existed before I started was non-existent.

I was also satisfied to know from some of the movie stars I was working with that they too had self-doubt and worry the first week or so as well. This was even more understandable considering that they know the movie production ultimately sits on how well they do or don't do their job in it. It doesn't matter how much experience one has under their belt because there will be some measure of self-doubt and worry that creeps in here and there.

The best you can do is to give it your best. I've

always given until it hurts when it's something I'm interested in. That's when you give and you give until you can't give anymore, but then you give more.

Let Go of the Obsolete

There comes a point when you have to come to the reality that you cannot continue to keep watering a dead plant. This metaphor can be applied to anything from relationships to your job. Perhaps you've done this with actual plants by continuing to water them long after they've wilted into the dirt. It's on its last leg and you're not giving up. You will continue to breathe life into it hoping to wake up one day and find that it's spruced back up again. There have been occasions where it miraculously strengthens and blossoms right back up out of nowhere. It's able to carry on for another six months to a year, but then it officially dies completely limp stuck to the dirt and you can't figure out what happened. It was like one day you wake up to find it's dead and probably had been for quite some time. The only regret is you allowed it to drag on longer than intended.

This is a metaphor to how you work on relationships and circumstances. How long will it take before you realize there is no life left in a connection or a situation? Know when it's time to wrap something up and bring it to closure. This way you may begin a new chapter with brighter blessings and circumstances dying to enter into your life. In order to bring in something great, you have to give up something of value.

You've permanently lost the passion for something or someone, but you relentlessly continue to beat that dead horse against a rock. You hang on longer than you should. You're exhausted by it, but you keep drowning that baby with water in hopes it will reverse its dormant behavior. I've seen others do this with someone they're in love with where they're not getting any mutual love and attention. They attempt to donate wasted time, effort, love, money, and energy into something that has no return. This also applies to work efforts and project endeavors, to staying in a work position you've been over with for a while.

I'm also way too loyal and I don't change, therefore I will stick with something or someone continuing to fight until I finally realize it's a lost cause. If you've done this too, then you understand when you look back that you may have allowed it to drag on much longer. As a loyal fighter you have the hope of some miracle turnaround. This can apply to love relationships where you can't make someone interested in you. They either are or they're not. You don't want to waste valuable time on people who are not your match.

Love and Forgiveness

All souls incarnate on Earth for the purpose of love, whether that is to learn to love, to teach love, to express love, or all of the above. As you've probably noticed many people haven't been able to master the basic art of love. This includes the ones that protest they love everybody. Attacking people over a statement that messed with your delicate sensitivities is not love.

The hyper technological age has seen a rise in instability and a lack of clarity and depth. The only way to change the hearts and minds of others is to show them goodness. Stomping around in a tantrum making all kinds of noise only expands that creating more noise. It changes no one and offers nothing positive.

Everybody is mad at everyone else for not living the way they want them to live. They're angry that someone else isn't graciously agreeing with what their ego wants. You're mad that someone else hurt you without apologizing. You've held onto that hurt for years allowing it to ensure it becomes a part of your consciousness refusing to let it go. You decline to forgive the person for what they've done so that you can move on. You reject the idea of letting go of the anger for what someone else chose to do. The person it's hurting in that equation is yourself. The other person is certainly not losing any sleep over it.

Don't worry about justice being served or not served because all karmic energy is paid back on some level. Let it go and forgive them so that you can be released from the burdens it's placed on your back crushing you into the ground. It's stalled you from moving forward into the next chapter of your life with a brighter, rejuvenated, awakened, transformed, and renewed outlook.

Be like the egoless angels, filled with an all-consuming love and forgiveness shining God's rays of light down onto all those void of love and in great need of healing and clarity. In their eyes, you are loved without judgment. It is the darkness of human ego that harshly judges others. This doesn't mean that someone committing cruel crimes on someone else will receive a free pass of forgiveness, but in Heaven's eyes you are expected to correct poor choices. You are expected to ask for forgiveness and to correct any wrongs you've been enacting on someone else. This is part of developing a deeper conscious. Partaking in wrongdoing knowing you'll be forgiven doesn't count, since that deceptiveness is taken into consideration. It's like giving someone a gift with the hopes of getting something in return. This isn't authentic giving when you desire something back.

If you continue making choices that negatively affect you or another, then you'll notice the ripple effect of adverse energy roaring through your life creating even more issues until you snap out of it and realize that the way you've been living isn't working. When you ask the bigger questions, then you receive the bigger answers. You grow more open to the art of learning and evolving. Moving from a toxic monster to a centered Light takes enormous willpower, because your ego will do everything it can to hold you down. It will do whatever it can to ensure your soul doesn't rise up into the Light.

The Darkness of ego and the Devil are one in the same. It rules Earthly life with an iron fist working through so many people on the planet pushing them to cause some form of harm, hurt, or hate filled act on others. It will push someone behind a computer screen to post daily negative based words all over the Internet through social media and websites that allow comments and posts. It will cause you to act out against your soul's better nature. It brings out the Devil in some of the worst ways imaginable. There was a time when physical violence reigned supreme. While it still exists, the new violence that rules Earthly life is through words, thoughts, and feelings. This is how the Darkness does his work, which is through poisoning the soul. He knows this energy moves rapidly able to bring out the greatest darkness imaginable out of the once purest Light. His goal is to bring everyone down as quickly as possible. He's been successful at it for so many centuries. Become the example of love, goodness, respect, and light. This is what always wins in the end.

You were born a pure Light of love, peace, joy, compassion, and understanding. You were filled with immense passion and love for all you came across. Throughout the soul's journey on Earth, it is faced with temptations, judgments, and harm by those around it that primarily function from the darkness of ego. It is your job to remember who you are and who you were when you were born out of God's love. It is one of your purposes and missions to rise above the hatred, darkness, and lower energies that assault you everyday. Move back into being the centered Light that you were made in.

Pay attention to the moments when you find you've become guilty of being a toxic monster. Climb out of that painful abyss as quickly as possible. Extricate the cause that triggered you to fall for the dark one's deception. Kick it out of your life for good. Don't forget who you are. You were born perfect in His love's Light. You have the power at your fingertips to create the most splendid magnificent life by the vibrational energy of your thoughts.

Move out of fear and toxicity by closing your eyes, taking a deep breath in, feel and experience His love light moving into and through you allowing it to become one with you. You have a centered Light within you that is waiting and willing to be ignited whenever you allow it. Make that choice today to become one with it once again. You have arrived in God's economy when you become a blessing to others. You are simultaneously becoming a blessing to yourself as well too.

When the lower energies and Darkness attempts to drown you in its dumps, then learn to pull yourself back up and climb out of that. Achieve laser focus by honing in on God and His Light. Rise up, stand tall, strong and centered in His grace. Revert back to the Light through regular prayer and faith that all will be well in the end. The more you do that, then the easier it becomes, and the less challenging life is as a result. You take things in better stride. Let go of the things you cannot change and positively alter and modify the situations that you can. Re-adjust the direction you were headed down and get back on that road that leads you towards your soul's purpose and goal. Rise above the mundane, physical, and superficial. Dive right back into the higher vibrational joy of your life. This life you've been blessed to have without losing sight of the grander Divine truths that are accessible within you.

CHAPTER ELEVEN

*Rise Above the Mundane
and Into the Divine*

Food and water are essential to human survival, but it is also common to rob yourself of much needed soul nourishment. Regularly hydrate your soul the same way you hydrate your body with water. The human race is trained early on to avoid putting themselves in the dramatic circumstance where they could be without water or food, even though many around the world suffer in this impoverished state with no evidence of Light at the end of that tunnel. It's easier for the masses to mobilize to protest or raise money for politicians or to voice their disapproval of a politician, but strangely nothing of such massive protest is ever made for causes such as child abuse or feeding the hungry. Food and water depravation cause grave damage to the physical body. Partaking in any kind of unhealthful activities for a consistent prolonged period amount of time will also do harm to the physical body. This simultaneously has an effect on the deterioration of the soul. When you nourish your physical body, then this has an effect on your state of mind and body.

God and all higher spirit beings love all souls equally and no one is ever ignored even when it feels that way. To Heaven, Earthly life is a blip on the radar, a millisecond compared to eternity. The perspective Spirit has is greater than imagined by the human mind. Experiencing that great love feeling from the Divine begins by increasing your faith and having regular daily prayer or conversations with God. Even if it feels like you're talking to no one, you are heard and responded to at some point. This is where you pick up on the messages and guidance immediately or further down the line. Sometimes you have to endure a rough patch before the light is shown. At the moment when the light appears, you realize why you were kept in a situation longer than you intended to be. This is that awakening moment when it all suddenly makes sense.

None of these statements are enlightening verbiage on a teabag for the soul. I can personally attest that the things I've asked for intervention or assistance with either came to me immediately or in the future on the outstretched wings of an angel. This means there have been circumstances that took years to transpire into fruition, but they did eventually emerge. I wouldn't feed anything to anyone that I hadn't experienced firsthand.

There were years that felt like an eternity wondering if something I desired would ever take place, but I believed in my gut that it would because I could also clairvoyantly foresee it visually in motion. This was the same foresight I'd see other things that would take place. It would eventually transpire and come to fruition. The question was always when.

A great deal of fearless confidence, persistence, patience, and progression were necessary traits to adopt.

Pray for a strengthening in faith when you feel like giving up and throwing in the towel. Ask for Heavenly help daily and believe you are heard. Request they help boost your spirit's fearlessness and bring you into the vortex of soul confidence. Pay attention to any guidance that could be coming in that is advising you on what to do. Praying, affirming, and asking for help daily is part of the equation, but so is taking action. It's that latter action step that many seem to ignore. They believe if they ask for help that they can then sit down and watch television until what they're asking for comes crashing through the ceiling and onto the couch next to them. You are expected by Heaven to put in the work as well too. It's not their job to sprinkle down blessings and gifts every single time you ask for something.

Can you imagine if a child was constantly asking their parent for a toy or a gift every single day? If the parent obliged to those requests, then they would have a spoiled child on their hands. That child will go through life expecting everything to be taken care of for it. When this doesn't happen, then a tantrum breaks loose, which is essentially what you're witnessing when some hide behind a computer or phone screen typing out words in an outrage on social media. It is impossible to have any clarity or psychic foresight when one is living on social media absorbing every bit of trending information and news story broadcast into your consciousness. It is designed to manipulate and hook you in, which it does successfully.

When you take a step away, then you are able to easily move into operating from your highest self's state of joy, peace, and love. That's when you are able to pick up on the divinely guided communication sifting in. You're also able to notice the Divine signs that indicate you're not alone and that you are loved and looked out for. In the physical world, the ego requires physical concrete material evidence of that love, but the love is felt from within like a great big warm hug. This is part of what having faith entails. There is nothing you can do to rescind that love. Spirit will not suddenly say, "Oh you're hopeless I'm done with you."

They function like good parents guiding and pushing you to become an independent soul by doing things yourself, while occasionally stepping in to help when it's gravely needed. They are your partners in this life.

As challenging as it is to believe even the most

heinous human being is loved. It is who the soul is deep inside that is loved. The intention is that the soul learns to reduce, dissolve, and limit operating from the darkness of ego. It is expected to awaken its consciousness to the spiritual reality they are bigger than the limited being they've chosen to confine themselves to. Heaven doesn't expect one to completely eliminate the darkness of ego, because even the most all loving and compassionate being on the planet will fall into the dark side on occasion. It's a limited rare occurrence that creeps up infrequently compared to the heinous dark human beings that have chosen to live a life ruled primarily from the darkest depths of their ego.

The dangers of a soul operating from the darkness of ego full time throughout its Earthly life run are that upon passing away the soul can get stuck in purgatory limbo between the Earth and Heaven plane or pulled into the back gate. This is no place to hang out where you run the risk of reliving bad Earthly experiences over and over again. The souls in limbo also make up some of the dark souls that attempt to attach themselves to Earthly loving souls. They will wreak havoc on that person's life or drive them to a toxic addiction. This could be the same addiction that the dark soul once formed a cord with while living in a human body. Your body will one day disintegrate into the physical Earth, but your soul consciousness remains as it was upon the physical death, only now it's liberated and free from confinement.

To sense the encompassing love from the Divine it is necessary to reduce Earthly distractions in order to raise the voices of Heaven. Participate in a soul detox that includes limiting technological use on certain days, getting out in nature to clear the mind, exercising regularly, reducing toxic foods and drinks, and centering and balancing out your thoughts and feelings. I know that sounds like quite a bit of work just to hear God. I can hear the grumblings of some saying, "I'm not doing all that. I'd rather that everything I need just land in my lap while I relax nursing a margarita while YouTube channel surfing."

Use discipline when it comes to what or who you allow into your world. Your world is you as well as everything around you. Your body should be treated with amazing care. It's a temporary home you're renting, which needs to be taken care of and cleaned like any property you rent. Avoid gossip, negative news, and the media swirling around you when feasible. Detach and unplug anything and everything when possible. Get out into nature to clear your aura regularly. Shun getting caught up in time wasting drama that stalls you from moving forward. Have self-discipline to avoid time wasters in general. This is especially when you need to get to work on important matters that may include your life purpose goals, to connecting with others in healthy personal relationships for physical experience and soul growth.

Personal and Work Life Balance

How is your work life balance? There are far more people on the planet today than there were pre-technology days. This means more cars and traffic on the roads than there used to be. Work lives have grown busier and demanding due to technology. It's become easy to send a work email to someone off hours and expect someone to dive into work on it or to respond. Boundaries no longer exist as to what's appropriate work etiquette because everyone is doing it and not able to be strict about not doing it unless it's an emergency, then you move into what constitutes an emergency. When there is a small break to get away from that, no one wants to hop in the car and sit in traffic for an hour to have a lunch with someone they haven't seen in awhile. Universally we've become comfortable in the new rut of the way things are. Often, it's not done on purpose, but the masses have moved in that direction as a collective.

Someone sends a work email and they're red flagging it like it's an emergency. You look at it and read it wondering, "This isn't urgent. Why would you red-flag this?"

The mentality process of the way people work has been altered in a way that there isn't a centered balance calm in the reign of chaos. Some people are so used to living and functioning stressed out that they carry this over to every aspect of their life. Everything that goes on is blown up and out of proportion to what the issue is. They're on edge filled with perpetual stressed out anxiety that everything is urgent, when most things are not as insistent as they make it. Most everything is fixable no matter what it is. How you move through something that needs to be corrected determines how efficient you are in a crisis.

I've communicated with people who head straight home after work because they're too exhausted to go out after being up since 6:30 am. They end up going home to continue working, since they receive work related email into the night by others who have nothing else to do. They don't know about incorporating boundaries and balance. Boundaries and balance are mandatory well-being traits that are mostly never taught to each person growing up by their parents, caregivers, teachers, or society.

Luckily with the rising interest in spiritual concepts there are armies of light workers that continue to expand and grow in numbers. They are interested in anything that helps improve overall life on Earth and individual well-being traits. This is knowing that incorporating self-care balance into your world can greatly extend your life span. They will pass this onto their children if they have them. Those children will pass it on to their own and so forth. Over time a mighty movement wave of peace, balance and love energy will pervade the planet with greater magnitude. It takes many generations to start noticing the positive effects.

When you love what you do, it doesn't feel like work, and therefore you keep on trucking not realizing how much of the day has passed. In those cases, you're not immune to experiencing burn out and should attempt to incorporate some form of balance and breaks. This also helps give you more energy, clarity, and focus that can be positively applied to your business.

Design and structure your life where you are able to balance work and play. This means you are putting in an equal amount of work, as you are to letting loose, playing, and relaxing. Playing and relaxing are as essential as getting to work. Working too much will cause burn out and the suffocation of great ideas, but playing too much and not getting to work promotes an idle slacker mentality. Find the happy medium between knowing when it's time to get to work, and when it's time to put the work down to have some much-needed fun.

The noise and chaos that exists in the media around you change nothing and offer no success. It only expands that energy making circumstances bigger than they are in reality. Having worked with and knowing some publicly known people, I've seen the media and news reports of them that blow something false up to the size of a skyscraper. Yet, when I'm with them everything is calm and relaxed, nothing at all is close to how the media portrayed them to be. It's astonishing to see how wide that fictionalized account of them in the media is compared to being in the room with them on a personal level. They are just like anybody else I know except they happen to have a job in this lifetime that has propelled them to popularity in the media. Early on I could never figure out what propelled the journalist or blogger to come up with the lie they printed. We know it was to ultimately entice viewers and stay in business. They know deep down that the public's dark ego loves drama. Sell drama or fear and you'll be a success! This works because so many people buy and believe it all.

One of the goals of the ego is to blindside and distract. It's been effective with that on a global scale. It will not give an opposing view a flash of insight, nor will it enlighten. That energy isn't designed to sway anyone, but is intended to add to the noise. It deludes you to believe it's changing something until time passes and you look back on that incident and realize it changed nothing. Those that believe otherwise do so to be able to justify behaving badly.

I've never personally been able to get or understand the nature of Twitter for example, but I know some around me love it. Scanning it in the past all I saw were people moaning and whining about something they hate, or they were attacking someone they hate. Doesn't sound like a phenomenon of mind-blowing information, but seems to allow the darkness of ego a playground to create additional unnecessary gossip, noise, and chaos. Even more disconcerting was how much attention those that spread that kind of darkness were getting. I've attempted to use it on occasion to post up words of messages, guidance, and wisdom, which is typically unpopular because it's not attacking anyone. The majority of users tend to get high off drama, which is why they log-on in the first place. This isn't to say that every user does that, but it has been noticed that it seems to be in the higher percentage ranges. I need tons of time to discuss an issue or topic. I've never been able to successfully reduce what needs to be said into a limited character sound bite. When I did try that I found that it was misunderstood, because it's not enough information to dive in-depth to dissect an issue to a level that is Universally clear. It's got to the point where social media is now primarily used to crucify someone publicly because you don't agree with them. There is a judicial system and a court of law for that.

Compromise, cooperation, balance, and tolerance are what modify an opposing perception. It's meeting others halfway and seeing their point of view and goal while lovingly getting them to see your view through understanding and compassion even if they disagree.

The saying that states *let's agree to disagree* is a repetitive statement that one should use more often. It's to say, "I know we don't agree on this particular topic, but I respect you and your point of view, so let's move onto other things.

A toxic monster would never dream of saying something like that. It will continue to attack, threaten, raise its voice, and stomp its feet in a tantrum until you succumb into submission and bow to its whim and join it. Stories that move up the trending charts are the ones where the lynch mob demands that someone apologize for something they said. When and if the recipient makes a public declaration of apology, then it's found to not be good enough and the attacks continue on relentlessly. It could be bemusing to see people live comfortably in that permanent toxic state of mind. Imagine knowing someone like that personally. How is that an enjoyable connection? There is no shred of light, reason, or psychic clarity in those spaces. It is to live and reside in a suffocating darkness that will only continue beyond death. I've met people that have fallen into that abyss and they're miserable grumps in general about everything. There is always some kind of drama or negativity going on in their life on any given day. The way I clairvoyantly see someone infected is there are a mixture of dark cords and webs entangled around them. There are also disgusting creepy crawlies moving about over them that are seeping in from the darker part of the spirit world. It's a sad and horrifying sight to witness that which they cannot see that's on them.

Emotionally detach from chaotic events to come to a higher understanding of the greater picture seeing all sides like a balanced judge. Focus on love and your higher self's path knowing that all will result well in the end.

I've always trusted the Divine guidance coming in because it has never failed me. It has been consistently and dangerously accurate regardless if it's the popular view or not. I don't pay any attention to what's common in current Earthly fads, and nor do I care. While others have fallen into the black hole abyss of what's being fed to them, I have continuously stood outside of it clear minded and focused as if viewing it through a glass wall in front of me. One could easily fall into the deepest suffocating madness of human world events. Spirit trained me not to be swayed by the human illusion presented. If I did that, then there would have been no reason to come here since that would mean I'm not ready or strong enough to withstand that dark energy.

Don't allow negativity and drama to sway you from your purpose. You become a way shower and a leader by inspiring and enlightening others, as well as remembering to display assertive love and compassion. Don't forget who you are and why you are here.

The toxic monster receives a rushed high by absorbing negative energy. Once consumed by it, you're yanked even deeper into the dark void drowning into its web of deceit. Be a warrior of light who shines so much light, confidence, and love onto all sides that your body cannot contain it. Remain neutral and balanced steering clear of the noise.

The human experience can bring on extremely intense days. The intensities that wreak havoc on your life are generally human driven. This is either by your own fear-based thoughts or actions. It can be someone else's words or actions around you that ultimately cause distress to your comfortable world. How you choose to take in those actions is up to you since no one on the planet can tell you how to think or feel about a situation.

Some temperaments are naturally prone to more fear or worry than another person. Anything that isn't human made or motivated is not going to cause much of a damper except for the occasional shifts and changes in the Earth's climate that can cause weather disasters. Other than that, most drama is human related, so it boils down to how you choose to accept or react to something.

Some personalities may be more dramatic than others in reacting. When there is a fire drill, it is how you choose to move through it that matters. When anyone is dramatic, then that will have a ripple effect creating anxiety and stress in those around you. When there is a catastrophe, people feel safer and comfortable with someone present that is strong, cool, and proactive to resolve an issue. Many police officers or security guards tend to fit that personality. Those guys also tend to be Knights incarnated to another Earthly life drawn to job career positions where those gifts are best utilized.

The movement of the planets in the Heavens has influence on the energy on Earth, since all energy is connected. It's not planets that make things happen, but it is how someone chooses to react on a day when the energy is testy. How you choose to move with that energy will determine how smooth you'll glide through a circumstance.

Some people see being governed by the planets as nonsense, but those are also the same people witnessed to having a harder time navigating through the tumultuous waters when a planet is in a challenging position. They also haven't studied up on it to understand its nature, which is typically the reaction of human behavior. The ego will judge something without studying, diving in, or doing their homework on it. Reading a headline and an article doesn't equate to knowing or understanding what's going on.

Those living in nature or in the middle of nowhere have it down. I've taken retreats and been out in those majestic nature locales and there are no issues at all. It's permanently calming and uplifting without all the noise of human distractions that escalate when there are more people around. Having strong clairsentience, I can pick up on that humanity is chaotic in general thanks to the darkness of ego.

During a Mercury Retrograde planetary transit, I can be in a busy city slammed with people and notice rising intense energies all around where one thing after another goes wrong. I've been in vast spaces of nature with no people during a Mercury Retrograde and there are zero issues or intensity noticed. This is because there are no people around who don't know what the retrograde is or how to move through it in the right way.

If you battle mental health well-being issues, then you can still carry the turbulence with you into nature even if you're alone. The unsettling intensities are not as bad on you than if you were in a noisy crowd full of strong erratic feelings darting all over the place like weapons. Being in a nature atmosphere with little to no people will greatly reduce the emotional stress pending you're not reading or watching toxic media. You should be outdoors! Nature is a natural powerful healing medicinal remedy to help calm, relax, or lighten certain mental health issues, such as anxiety and depression.

CHAPTER TWELVE

*Cord Cutting, Shielding,
Grounding*

As you make positive life changes and adjustments that include modifications to your diet and your exercise routines, it is vital to be psychically aware when antagonistic energies are in your vicinity. Most people head to work on a daily basis only to be met with a colorful array of personalities. Some are good and some are shooting invisible daggers at you. If clairvoyance is your strong psychic sense, then you may see this energy. If you are clairsentient, then you are feeling what others are pouring into you as if you are a drainpipe for their pollutants.

There are techniques you can partake in that can minimize or eliminate the effects the damage causes you at the hands of others. You will need to keep an open mind about some of these methods described. Have trust and faith that it works, since these methods do and have worked for me and countless others. You need to be disciplined about it. You can always test my Guides and Angel's hypothesis before you discredit it. If you have an analytical mind that works in the same rational way mine does, then you may be skeptical about cord cutting. I've spoken with many others that were hesitant, but then decided to give it a try. They would report back to me later to say they started to notice positive changes and improvements in their lives after adopting some of these methods.

It can be challenging making the transition into a light worker or rising up into a warrior of light. Sometimes there are people in your life that hold you back from evolving. They get in the way, give zero support, or cause you grief. If there are certain people you wish would go away, then you can do so by what is called *cutting cords* or *cord cutting*. It is almost like magic in the way it astonishingly works.

Anytime you connect and form a relationship with or to someone whether that is a family member, friend, colleague, business or love relationship, you form an etheric cord of attachment to them. Clairvoyantly this looks like an etheric gasoline hose coming out of the other person and hooking itself onto you. For example, if the person is needy, negative, or always stressed out, then they are pulling high vibrational energy out of your soul. This feels as if someone is sucking the life force right out of you. This gasoline hose is actually a dark etheric cord that clairvoyantly looks like spider webs wrapped around this tube strangling it.

Whenever someone in your life affects you negatively, you can be sure you have a toxic cord attached to them. You will feel drained, stressed out or uncomfortable whenever they are around you. When the thought of them approaching you makes your stomach turn, then you can be sure you have a tough nasty cord connected to them.

This cord attachment is formed between romantic partners or potential dates as well. Let's say you are chasing a guy or girl who is not romantically interested in you. You start to check that person's social networking page daily for weeks. This is followed by a negative cord of attachment to that person. You grow to obsess over it to the point where it has taken over your life in an unhealthy way, which starts to darken this cord. Married couples, roommates, and anyone that lives together form cords of attachments. This is why some couples are so in tune to how the other is feeling. Both of the lights around your souls have connected and merged. The cord is still present even if one of you is living in another city. This is why you need to make sure that you and your partner are aiming to practice living a life of joy in your individual lives when possible, since you will have rough days just like anybody else. If one of you is experiencing constant negativity for months at a time, then the other partner will absorb that causing your cord between one another to become polluted. This is draining and can even cause you to have incessant arguments or to ultimately break up. One of the many points of a relationship is that you support and lift your partner up when they're experiencing discord.

It's important to cut cords regularly to certain relationships due to the buildup of dirty energy. This doesn't mean that you are cutting them out of your life necessarily unless this is what you choose. You are removing the dysfunction or toxic part of the relationship.

What I have discovered while cutting cords is that Archangel Michael will either remove and eliminate that person out of my life or improve the relationship. They eliminate them if they know there is no additional purpose or lessons needed to happen with that particular connection. Archangel Michael will remove the person in question if the lessons you need to gain with them are completed. They will also remove them if that person is still hanging around causing you turmoil. This can simultaneously hold you back from moving forward. Your vibration has risen while the other person remains buried under a lower vibration. They are not intending to deplete your energy, but this is what is happening regardless since you are made up of energy. If you are a sensitive person, then you are especially susceptible to the repercussions of forming an attachment to a negative and toxic person. I cut cords to certain people as part of my daily morning ritual. I mentally cut cords throughout the day if I need immediate cord cutting intervention with someone hostile or draining around me.

Sometimes when you work with certain toxic people, then it may be difficult to get rid of them. This is where some of the uninvited contamination in your aura happens. The second place is at home if you are living with others. This is why it is important to do your best to ask that you be guided to work or live with high vibrational people. If you are unable to live alone, request to live with similar higher vibrational people who are peace loving souls or to help alter the low vibrational person's frequency. You will need to raise your vibration and keep that energy in your vicinity in order to attract in someone of a high caliber. High vibrational people can sense someone who is not of integrity or who is going to be a problem from a mile away.

If you are in a loving, committed relationship with someone and you are living together, then you have formed a cord. If the relationship is based on 100% pure love and compassion, then the cord will not be as dirty, but there will be a cord. You still need to keep some form of detachment so as not to fall into a position of co-dependency since the cord can get dusty. Those that you have formed a cord attachment with are not purposely attempting to drain your energy or spit toxins into you. They are unaware they are doing this. You are your own barometer gauge to know how certain people affect you. This is your soul to protect and it is up to you to manage it. You have the assistance of God, your angels, guides, and archangels within reach for this process. All you have to do is ask for their help.

You don't need to chant some complex invocation. Saying something like this below has invited in heavenly help:

"Okay, Archangel Michael I need your help with this…"

As you begin cutting cords, then you will find methods that you're comfortable with that work for you. You can think the word "angels" and you are heard and have invited them in to help.

Say, *"Archangel Michael I call on you now. Please cut the cords between (so & so) and I."*

List the people that you find to be toxic and draining. Say one person's name at a time. Take a deep breath in and exhale after each name. Do this by visualizing Archangel Michael taking his light sword and slicing the cord away between you and this other person. The people you list are those you know you will have to deal with or face that day and you definitely do not want to. Sometimes it might just be one person while other times it's a few. There are some whom you will have to cut cords with every single day for months until they are gone from your life or the connection improves. When you find a connection is putting you in a repeated negative place, then cut the cords immediately. There are those you love and are close to, and you do not want them to go away, but you do not want any pain or dysfunction in your world anymore either. For those cases you could say something like this:

"Please cut the cords between (the person) and I. Only remove the toxic, fear and dysfunction from this relationship, but keep the love and

lessons."

When I've requested that the dysfunction be removed, I have found those relationships drastically improve or they elevate into something better. I hear Archangel Michael cutting the cords with one slash of his light sword. If it is a difficult cord that's hard as concrete, then he will continue cutting every day until it is removed. This can work with someone you're involved with romantically. If you find yourself not trusting them, and yet you have no valid proof to be reacting this way, then you will want to cut the cords with them. Some are afraid to do that because they fear that the person they love will be taken away. Having the cords cut does not necessarily mean they will be banished from your life. Your Guides and Angels will take care of the when and how. They will make the decision that benefits your higher self's path. All you need to do is ask for assistance. There is no reason to endure negative insecurities with anyone including a romantic partner.

I have had cases in the past where I was stuck having to deal with someone I did not want around me. This might have been an acquaintance or colleague that was toxic, negative or a gossip - all of which I will have no part of. It was pushed to the point where I was done with them. I had no interest and they offered nothing to me in the way of progress or growth, but merely contributed to heightened negative feelings. For those special cases I am quite firm in my cord cutting and even angry if nothing has been done about it. The angels are egoless and see your true light and nature. They don't take anything personally such as you stomping your feet in aggression. Not that I'm advocating that you do that, but there have been times where you are pushed to the edge and scream out for help.

"That's it! I want you to cut the cords between (the person's name) and I. Remove them from my life in all directions of time. Thank you."

I will immediately begin to see that our connection is elevated to a level that I can tolerate, or they are removed from my life permanently.

With some suspects, it can take a while to remove them out of your life, but you need to cut cords to them every single day. Do not give up or stop cutting cords until you feel the circumstance has improved. I have witnessed incredible results over the course of my life doing this for myself or I would not continue with it.

Sometimes it's a process to extricate some people out of your life. The improvement might not be right away. I have witnessed changes and shifts happen over a period of time for some cases. Suddenly that person is let go from their job, they decide to leave and move on, or you have been moved away from them. The angels are maneuvering obstacles in the way. This is in order to bring about the changes you wish for that benefits your higher soul. They might be working behind the scenes with the other person's guardian angels to enact positive changes that benefit all parties involved. In the meantime, continue cutting those cords to that person every day until they are gone, or you are seeing an improvement in your connection with them.

Working lower energy jobs while attempting to grow your light and become spiritually evolved can be challenging. You might have to deal with someone that can be disconnected from the real reality and living in full on arrogant ego mode. They are extremely deadly to you, your environment, and well-being. You could be working at the greatest place on Earth with wonderful colleagues, but there might be one or two bad apples who you might love to toss out a window. Every time you turn around, they are standing there. They might be pushing your buttons in a negative way or getting under your skin. This is where cutting cords works beautifully. These are people you have to cut cords to every single day. They may not always be extricated from your life immediately, but you will start noticing them become a bit more tolerable and eventually off your radar. You form a cord of attachment to anything that is made up of energy. This means that cords can also be formed with material items such as your home, car or any other material items that you hold dear to your heart. You form cords to your feelings and emotions too. Cord cutting is a positive lifestyle trait you're adopting and incorporating regularly. Be aware of what you are attached to, as that is a clue as to where the cords exist.

If a loved one has crossed over to the Other Side, your cords are still connected. This is the case if you had a strong tie on Earth. These energetic cords that both departed spirits and human souls share. Cord attachments are not always negative, but they can be. You would know if the cord has turned dirty. You might feel weighted down or lethargic when you think of that person. You feel negative thoughts or anxiety when that person is on your mind. This is a sign that their energetic cord is attached to you. You would need to cut the cords with that person, especially if it is preventing you from functioning or moving forward.

There is no difference whether the cord is connected to someone on the Earth plane or in the spirit world. It is an etheric cord connecting two souls. Your soul can have hundreds of cords attached to it since there is no limit. However, it is unlikely one would have that many at one particular time because you would feel it and know it. Your mind is not thinking of hundreds of people at once. If someone has not been on your radar for some time and you have had no communication for years, then it is not likely you would have a cord attached to that person since it has dissolved away over time. Unless this is a rare circumstance where you have been thinking of this person every day since.

These cords attached to someone else can be communication devices with that person. This is why married or committed couples for example know and sense what is going on with their partner without them uttering a word. The same goes for exes. I have communicated with exes and old friendships telepathically on occasion in the past. This was long before I controlled my thoughts.

This communicating with them telepathically prompted them to reach out to me. Call on Archangel Michael to cut those cords daily.

These etheric cords grow and form between yourself and any object you place your focus on whether positive or negative. This object can be people, material items, or your thoughts and feelings. When you become attached to any of those things and it is bathed in negativity, then a cord is formed between yourself and the point of your focus. A dirty cord drains your life force and lowers your vibration, especially if it's negative. Not only do you lose the object of your focus due to the blocks erected as a result of your negative feelings, but it delays you from moving forward and brings in more negativity from other areas. It grows like a wild and unruly fire.

If you have constant disagreements with someone, then your connection with them becomes toxic. This is a sign that it is time to cut the cords between yourself and this other person. No one benefits in going back and forth to rehash an issue with anyone where two people are not compassionately seeing one another's differing point of view. This doesn't only apply to friendships, but rifts on social media between strangers not agreeing over a certain viewpoint. Calling people names because they have a separate view is not going to suddenly wake them up. This lowers both you and the other person's vibration while creating a cord attached to them. Who wants an etheric cord attached to an enemy?

Constructively explain to someone with

compassion that hating anyone who is not like you is more likely to open their mind rather than sending a tirade of attacks. It also raises your vibration because you're coming at it from a place of love, then let it go, walk away, cut the cords and move on.

When you think about someone and your thoughts move to upset, depression, sadness, anger, or any other negative feeling, then you have formed a dark cord to this person. You pine over someone you have interest in, but become dejected when you come to the realization that they're not succumbing to your interest. This is a sign you have formed a dark cord to this other person. No love exists within that cord. This is why it is imperative to have those etheric cords cut.

Cutting cords does not always remove this person, so there is no need to fear that you will lose the person after you cut the cords. The only time the person is pushed away or removed is when your Spirit team knows that this connection is not beneficial to your higher self's goal in any way. In the end, the removal of this person or object is for good reason, such as they might have been abusive. Sometimes you have to walk away from someone you love because you know that the connection is toxic. There are no benefits for anyone in a connection like that. It endures the drama preventing you both from moving forward in your lives. You do not want ten years to go by when you realize how much time you wasted not letting that person go.

Cut the cords to anyone or anything that is

toxic, not of love, or of benefit to your higher self's path. If you're wondering what cords you need to release, then examine the negative emotions you're feeling around anyone or anything. Are you feeling sad, depressed, argumentative, stressed, or angry? Whatever the upset is targeted to is a clue as to what you need to release. Let it all go, release it, or let them go. When you cut the cords and release it, then you open the door that brings in new good stuff! You also feel an uplifting surge of positive energy that raises your vibration.

Archangel Michael is the go-to higher being for cord cutting, but you can call on the Heavenly being or guide that you are most comfortable with. You can call on God, Jesus, or Buddha to cut the cords. Any higher being in Heaven can assist in getting these cords cut. If it's a stubborn issue, then you cut the cords to that object every single day until you intuitively sense that all is well again. If you work or go to school with that one person that rubs you the wrong way, then every morning as you begin your day, request that the cords be cut between you and this person.

Sometimes you're unaware that you've formed a cord with someone else. When you experience negative emotions over anyone or anything, then you're no longer seeing a situation clearly. The road up ahead is filled with a hazy fog that blinds you from reality. Perhaps you're hoping the object of your affections will return your interest, but none is given. This causes you to feel depressed and upset. A dirty damaging etheric cord has now wrapped around your soul and hooked itself onto this other person's soul. Cutting these cords releases the negativity associated with this cord. You do not need to be around someone who is constantly disrespecting you and causing drama. It's not worth it in the end when there are many wonderful peace-loving people in the world.

Cutting cords is a beneficial tool you can utilize daily when it comes to enhancing your soul. Your life could be a busy stress packed one where you're surrounded by energies that contaminate your aura regularly. This is where cutting cords can assist. You can cut cords to a former faith-based religion that was toxic to you. Some religious teachings within certain faiths have nothing to do with God. They instill traits in you such as fear, guilt, harm, or low-self-esteem. Those traits are dark ego teachings and not God teachings. You can be part of any faith you're interested in delving into. You will draw your own conclusions as to what feels right to you when it comes to what others are sharing. Bringing you closer to God should never be done by making you feel bad about who you are. True, honest, faith based spiritual teachings will have love and compassion with it.

Cutting the cords to family, loved ones, or those who have been close to you are the most difficult cords to cut. You can cut the cords without cutting them out of your life. It's the dysfunction that's cut. Sometimes you have to nip it in the bud and say enough is enough. It's time to cut the cords to this person or situation. My life is intended to be peaceful and not stressful.

Shielding

Follow the cord cutting ritual by asking God and Archangel Michael to shield you with protective white light allowing only those of love to be allowed to penetrate it.

I am a sensitive that grew to have immense social anxiety due to a volatile violent upbringing. With the help of my Spirit team I was able to bring my social anxiety down to a manageable level. I was also born and raised and functioning in an unpredictable and somewhat soulless city like Los Angeles. You take unstable people and give them a machine to roam around in and control, such as a car, then you have a full-blown battlefield on the streets. The energy is worse than the anger of a murdering terrorist. This isn't just my perception, but other Los Angeles natives have said the same thing. And now there are statistics citing Los Angeles as the #1 city with the most aggressive drivers in the United States. This is why it is important to shield yourself wherever you are.

Shielding is another beneficial process to incorporate especially if you are a sensitive person. Sensitive people absorb more energy emanating off of others like a muddy kitchen mop.

Take a deep breath in and exhale out. Call upon God and Archangel Michael. Ask him to shield you with bright white light for protection. Visualize a cocoon of white light surrounding you. This will keep out those nasty pests that insist on entering your field. The people you work for or whom you are around regularly can be the greatest people, but even great people get moody, agitated and out of line. You sense this energy and vibration and it suddenly lowers yours. See the innocence and humor in other people, and do not let their drama and moods affect you. Be wary of over shielding yourself or your business to the point where all are invisible unless that's what you choose. To avoid that from happening ask Archangel Michael to surround you with a white shield of light allowing only the love to infiltrate.

You can request and envision different colored shields of light around you as well too. These heavenly lights can be layered together or on its own. Your soul and aura is six feet tall, which is why your soul is literally too big for your body. It is important to be aware of it, sense it, and take care of what enters your auric field. The shields of heavenly light last up to twelve hours so you will need to do it daily as needed.

Cord cutting and shielding needs to be done daily when desired because the shielding fades after twenty-four hours. Cutting cords daily between yourself and a problem you're unable to remedy can benefit. The cords will dim or grow darker depending on the toxic people you come into contact with. Do this daily until you notice positive changes happening. It will be done with your higher self's best interest at heart. The connection will gradually begin to improve, or one day you'll find the person has decided to move away. It ends up being a blessing in disguise after they've gone away leaving you to discover you're officially at peace.

Light Shielding with Meanings

- White – Strongest light that protects you. Nothing can penetrate this shield.

- Rose/Pink – Offers protection while allowing only the love to enter your auric field.

- Emerald Green – Heals you in all ways such as physically, mentally or emotionally.

- Violet – Assists in raising your spiritual gifts and psychic sight.

- Gold – Incredibly powerful. Brings in God's love and light. Blasts away and repels all traces of negative thoughts and your lower self from your mind and body.

Grounding

Grounding is the process of connecting your soul to the physical world. You can lose yourself if you float too far upwards into the next plane. While this can be exhilarating, it is helpful to find the right balance between the spiritual world and the physical world. Grounding into the physical world helps you reap the benefits of the material world. This isn't saying to desire an overindulgence in material possessions, but there is nothing wrong with obtaining material necessities for your human survival such as a home, family, food, clothing, car, etc. When you're not grounded, you can be feeling out of sorts, chaotic, anxiety ridden, or unfocused. Grounding helps you balance that out so you're clear minded, focused, and full of life.

In order to ground your soul, find a place anywhere in nature, whether it's a park, beach, desert, mountain, or your own backyard. Connecting with physical nature helps to ground you. You can take a walk through these areas and breathe in deeply and exhale. Ask your Guide and Angel to work on grounding you while strolling through a nature setting. Take your shoes off and allow your body to connect with the Earth by planting your bare feet on the ground. This can be in the sand, on a beach, or on the grass in a park. Visualize white light moving from below the Earth, and up through your feet, then through your body, and out through the top of your head. Take deep breaths in and exhale out any stresses, worries, or cares by releasing it all out into the heavens.

Finding an area with little to no people if possible is extra effective, because you don't have the tampering energies of the noise of the crowds. It's perfectly fine to be with a loved one or calming friend who is looking to chill out in nature and connect as well. Lean your back up against a tree and allow the Earth's healing properties to work its way through your spirit. Working on a garden outside also helps to ground you. You're moving your spirit light into the Earth's light as you work your hands into the physical world. This merges the physical and spiritual part of you. The key is the contact between the physical earth and your physical body. Both simultaneously connect with your spiritual body and light, which assists in igniting your inner life force.

It is essential to ground and vital for the well-being of your overall health. Grounding is connecting with nature and the physical Earth. It can be walking barefoot in nature or anywhere the Earth can touch your skin, such as the woods, grass, lake, or beach. Grounding is helpful in obtaining a stronger frequency connection with your Spirit team. It's more than just putting your feet on the soil. It's planting your feet on the ground while sitting or standing. Close your eyes and feel and visualize tree roots wrapping around your feet and growing downward into the ground. Take at least a few minutes or longer if you prefer to do this.

There have been scientific tests conducted on individuals who were considered to be unhealthy. The test required them to go barefoot in nature to connect to the physical Earth. They used an infrared test that exposed them as they grounded. It showed that before they began grounding the cells in their body were dark. As they grounded, the dark cells lightened and showed fewer of them in the test subject's bodies. This isn't surprising since all living souls and organisms are made up of cells and energy that is constantly shifting depending on your lifestyle and those you surround yourself with.

Grounding assists in giving you a stronger

connection with the Other Side. Close your eyes, inhale deeply, and then exhale. Do this exercise several times until you feel relaxed. Then, as you're continuing to inhale, imagine you are inhaling bright white light. As you inhale this light, allow it to move through your body and consume all of you inside and out. Exhale breathing out this light so that it is surrounding your body and growing larger. You might feel a little dizzy or lightheaded while grounding and connecting. This is releasing toxins out of your body and replacing it with Heavenly light. You are having high psychic input where it's bouncing all over the place. This is whether or not you hone it or take classes to keep the hypersensitivity at bay. Grounding can certainly help to bring your soul back down to earth. Have one foot in this world and one in the other.

Cutting cords, shielding, and grounding is a lifestyle you're adopting to ensure you travel along your path as serene as possible.

CHAPTER THIRTEEN

Vibrational Uplift

Millions of people around the world acknowledge holidays, their birthdays, or even the end of the year as a guide to see how far they have improved or progressed. They look at it as a time out to celebrate with optimism in hopes that the future will be brighter for them. It is when people will often say, "Next year will be better."

If you keep saying tomorrow will be better, then you will always be one step away from happiness. Feel peacefulness today and then your challenges will lessen.

You are being asked to examine your life in a deeper way in order to make significant positive changes. Many human souls have been waking up in the process. This transformation you have been going through will make the ego unhappy, because change is something different than what you are accustomed to. You get uncomfortable whenever there is a drastic adjustment that forces you out of your comfort zone.

There is often fear energy talk surrounding new diseases or an end of the world. These are all false fads that are beat upon society by human ego. There is never going to be an end of the world, but the negativity and the obsessive focus on that sort of talk amplifies the darker sides of the world's character.

Get unstuck so you can be at a place that benefits your soul. Evaluate your beliefs, values and ways of doing things and make significant changes in your life immediately. Shed all of that garbage from in and around you. This will open you up to be receptive to the wonderful circumstances headed your way. Be open to receive those gifts in the right spirit and start living fully today.

Daydream

Avoid getting caught up in the noise and drama of the world's often dark nasty behavior. Human drama flies out from all angles on a regular basis. It is erratic and unstable. It does nothing to help you or anybody. Take regular time outs than necessary and relax and smile more. Shun going to places where you know it is going to be taxing on your system. Go for walks alone, or with a love interest or friend, and daydream. Do this in a nature setting if possible. Daydream about beautiful, wonderful circumstances and feelings.

Think about the amazing blessings you currently have and then daydream about what you would like to see manifest next in your life. If your life is where you want it, then daydream about that more. Take walks in areas where you know it will not be crowded with people. I've witnessed others attempting to go for a stroll in busy cities only to dodge restless and reckless drivers nearly running them over. You're on guard and your heart rate shoots up on high alert every time you have to cross a busy street with impatient drivers. I saw a child leaving school alone and running across the street in the crosswalk in a panic because it sensed that toxic energy coming off the drivers. This is no way to relax and center your soul. It was devastating to see that a child was so aware of it. Venture off into a nature setting whenever possible for strong effectiveness.

Find a quiet place to focus or meditate on anything that is not human made. This can be something like a sunset, a plant, flower, or mountain peak.

Full Moon

The moon phases and cycles have a larger energy power behind them. The New Moon is a great time to start a new positive activity or regimen. This can be things like beginning a new relationship, job, an exercise routine, to sending out your resume. The New Moon symbolizes new beginnings. The Full Moon has immense manifestation power as well. The Full Moon is typically a nice phase to release bad habits, things, or people, while aligning your focus with what you truly desire. The energy is so powerful that it can pull uncomfortable things out of you.

Release that which has been delaying you and holding you back from positive progress. You likely already know what you need to let go of, but are procrastinating out of fear or indecision. It is anything or anyone that brings you down or prompts you to experience consistent inadequate feelings such as depression, anger or stress. This also includes foods and substances that are not good for you and cause your body to react negatively such as giving you low energy or irritability. This delays you from taking positive action and in moving forward. Release anything negative so that you can truly be free and soar upwards to where your higher self lives. When you release negative stuff, then you are on your way to obtaining your dreams. Your dreams come true as a result of this release, but you have to do the work. You have to release negative thoughts, patterns, lifestyle choices and people.

The Full Moon transit is a great time for releasing, re-aligning and then manifesting positively - so watch your thoughts! Many use the night of the Full Moon to release that which no longer serves them or their higher self. You can do this mentally or write it down and burn the sheet safely. It's the intention that has the power. Release anything or anyone that you know is toxic and causes you to experience uncomfortable feelings. The energy of the Full Moon is potent, intense, and powerful. It brings up all sorts of feelings and thoughts. It has the force to magnify and direct your energy in large ways. This is why it is important to be crystal-clear with your thoughts in general, and especially on the night of the Full Moon.

Simply having intention can make this release happen efficiently. One way is by meditating or gazing upon the Full Moon for 5-15 minutes. Take a deep breath in, exhale, and repeat until you are fully relaxed. Breathe in and connect with the Moon so that you are one with it. You can do this longer than fifteen minutes if you choose. Sitting underneath the Full Moon outside in order to make contact with you is even better. Sometimes this is not realistic if it is a cloudy or rainy night, but as long as the intention is there is all that matters.

Mentally visualize what you would like to remove from your life. Follow that with what you would like to see come to fruition. This brings your Spirit team in by your side notating the work you are putting in to make healthy life changes. Archangel Haniel is the hierarchy angel who you can benefit from working with during that time. Ask her to be with you through the Full Moon releasing process. She awakens your third eye chakra which opens up clairvoyance.

The New and Full Moon transits add extra

manifesting energy to your thoughts. Be careful with your thoughts more than usual during those moon phases. Keep them positive and upbeat. If your mind goes into worry or something negative, then you are going to bring about more of that to you.

Check online or a planetary calendar for the dates of the New and Full Moon phases. Most calendars have those two transits listed each month.

Flowers

Flowers raise your vibration, so fill your surroundings with flowers. Purchase flowers or put up photographs of flowers. Having the real thing is the most beneficial. If the only option is a framed picture of a flower due to severe allergies or other circumstances, then that's better than no flowers. If you have allergies, call on Archangel Raphael and ask him to reduce or eliminate the severity of the allergies. Pay attention to the guidance he places in your path where other alternatives to having a flower can come into play.

Lean into the flower and breathe it in. If this is a photograph of a flower, then envision that it is real as you lean in to breathe it in. Notice how wide open the flower is with its arms outstretched. Take it all in allowing it to awaken and open up your mind and senses. Meditate on the flower or image and take a deep breath in. On the exhale release any negative thoughts or lower vibration words that you have been using. The flower's arms expand wide giving you a big hug.

The flowers, trees, plants, grass and all of nature are gifts from God to help you relax and connect with your Spirit team. God created flowers for numerous purposes. One of them is to surround you with beauty. Beauty and flowers both raise your vibration. It's a double whammy! It is not okay to destroy nature and this world through greed and naivety. Flowers keep this planet alive and to keep you feeling alive. Flowers are little reminders of the beauty that exists in the Spirit world, which is abundantly ripe with flowers. Nature is a powerful sense awakener with immense healing properties. When you take in a huge inhale of a flower, then your spirit feels invigorated. Your mind opens up becoming clear, focused, and stimulated. Absorbing nature regularly prompts you to experience the natural uplifting feelings of well-being.

Placing flowers around you can invite positive circumstances into your life. Each color tends to bring in specific energy into your vicinity. The darker the shade of that particular color, then the more intense it will be. The lighter the shade of that color, then the softer the energy will be. If it is a pink flower, then it can bring in more love into your life. If that pink is a deeper rose color, then the love will be heavier and more intense. The lighter the pink is in that flower, then the softer the love is or subtle it is.

Here is an example cheat sheet of the healing properties that the color of a flower can give off.

Place these flowers around your space if you would like to invite in a higher energy for a specific desire:

• Red – passion, romance, sexiness, deep relationships and commitments

• Pink – Love, beauty, attractiveness

• Yellow – Joy, optimism, success, ideas, positive thoughts, friendships

• Green – Healing, releasing, cleansing

• Violet – Spiritual awakenings, protection, third eye opening

• White – Harmony, Purity, vibration lifting, hope

• Orange – Growth, vibration raising, empowerment, expansiveness, career

• Blue – Strength, courage, calming, honor, creativity

Rainbows

The Rainbow colors are a mixture of colors that different hierarchy spirits exude and radiate. They are high vibrational colors and lights. Archangel Raziel shows up wherever rainbows or rainbow colors are. There is nothing negative or cryptic about a rainbow connection. They are reflections of light created as a message from Heaven. They are one way that someone on the Other Side is sending you a message if you are seeing the same symbol repeatedly. Heaven will communicate through repeated symbols and signs that have the same pattern. It would depend on what type of help you are asking for if any to decode those symbols.

If your question or request for Heavenly assistance were in regard to a work promotion or something having to do with material success, then the rainbow would be a sign that the pot of gold is coming up or good news is on the horizon. The rainbow can also be a bridge or a passage that things are looking up. It also means hope and assurance that God is indeed present. Whenever God is present it is always a reminder that you need to be exuding love more often. He is always present, but when He is showing signs of His bigger presence, then it would show up in many forms including rainbows. He does not reveal his presence through violent acts despite what some might believe. Those are the acts of human ego. God is all love.

Awaken Your Inner Child Through Joy

It is inevitable that you will hit a rough patch in your Earthly life. This might be where your soul feels lost, overly emotional, or lethargic. Sometimes these feelings signify that you are on the precipice of grand changes needing to happen in your life. It is a transformative period prompting you to be more introspective. What matters is how you work through the issues that this energy is bringing out of you. What it creates within you might be uncomfortable as it is asking you to examine where you are at in your life. This can be in any area such as career, relationships or health.

Learn from your current circumstances, choices and experiences. Avoid remaining mired in negative feelings and thoughts. Heavy emotions force you to be hyper-focused on where you are at. This prompts you to feel stuck as if you are trapped in an eternal prison. Uncomfortable feelings stall your progress and forward movement. It becomes difficult to reach a place of happiness while in that state.

In order to work through these feelings and thoughts, you have to examine them with a fine toothcomb. Look for the underlying cause and message that continues to prompt you to obsess over thoughts which have no basis in reality. What areas in your life are provoking you in a negative way? Those are areas which require a necessary change. Ask your Spirit team for assistance and follow their guidance even if they push you out of your element. Know they do this for your own higher self's good. It is a sign that it is a time to move on to the next plateau. See only the love and lessons in the experiences you are asked to modify or leave. Make your peace with it in order to move to a brighter, content life.

Inviting laughter into your life is crucial to your well-being. It opens up your heart while awakening and unleashing your inner child. It has profound health benefits next to love. Love and joy are two of the highest energy vibrations in the universe. The entire Spirit world is bathed in the wonders of exuding those powerful feelings eternally. These are some of the biggest most recurring messages I receive. The messages sound easy enough, but why is it so hard for some souls to live in that space 24/7? Many lives are full of stresses, toxins and disappointments. You have no problem living in those conditions and choosing grief instead of harmony. This way of living is thrust upon you by others. It is a learned trait because you certainly were not born that way. You come into contact with someone that is negative or toxic and you absorb that energy. You end up taking it out on someone else and they pay that forward and so forth. Your aura and soul darkens along with your state of mind. Soon you are behaving like that too. You pass it around to one another like contagion. This is what gets passed around when it should be lightheartedness, optimism, love and laughter. Many choose a path of deep anguish where they allow that distress to drop to a level where no one can reach them.

I sense every range of energy in the air without escape and we are indeed stressed globally. There are evolved souls in this lifetime spreading humor and joy, but it's not enough to get the tides moving fast enough. Get everyone to join in!

It can be challenging being around others who are permanently mired in negativity and you cannot get away from them. They may be a romantic partner, family member, roommates and the worst offenders, which are colleagues. The reason they are the worst offenders is because many people spend most of their days with those they work with. You cannot escape them. If that one draining apple exists in the bunch, they have the power to shift the entire mood within the work environment. Typically, that one sour grape is keen on spreading it around to others who are not interested. This causes a decline in productivity and morale. It takes great effort to raise it again. This is carried over into your daily personal life when you head outside, brave the streets, and eventually head home. You pass that energy to your friends and loved ones. You suppress it or feed it by getting your hands on a toxic addiction.

A friend sent me one of those fun social media tests that allow you to check to see what your mental age is. I scored the lowest in our group showing that my mental age is nineteen. I joked that I am either immature or young at heart. This is an example of keeping your responsibilities and commitments balanced, but also remaining young at heart. Take some time out daily to see the humor in life. Make light of situations that would otherwise be distressing. You might have put your body into a tense position, or perhaps you are stuck in a rut without realizing it. You can get unstuck if you remember to have fun and unleash your inner child. You remember that kid when it was little.

You saw the wonder and joy in the smallest things. When you laugh and have fun it opens up your heart Chakra, which not only invites romantic and loving situations into your life, but it also enables you to manifest your glorious dreams. The Heart Chakra is connected to Clairsentience, the psychic clair sense.

Do whatever it takes to get you to that place of feeling happy and content. This can be anything small from watching a funny, uplifting movie, to hanging out with a cheerful friend who always makes you laugh. Place your work and worries aside and celebrate your life. Be grateful for what you currently have. See your soul and where you're at in a positive light. See the blessings that you have in your life right now. Do not think about or worry over what is coming next or what is not here. Put that all aside and let loose and enjoy yourself. Learn to celebrate this life and insist on having more good times.

Get Unstuck from the Rut

Many around the world continue to feel stuck. They are in the middle of a transition or they're at a crossroads evaluating all aspects of their lives that cause unhappiness. They know changes need to take place in their lives. There is going to be quite a bit of moving on as far as changes go for them. Leaving one way of life and into another. This includes a great deal of people walking away from their current employment and into another one, or leaving one relationship and into another. Many will be making moves to improve their lives. This includes adopting a more balanced point of view.

It is time to work on getting unstuck and work on changing your perception of world events as well as personal ones. Incorporate positive healthy life changes and viewpoints. Tune into the higher vibrations of spirit to see the truth of why events and circumstances take place. Negative anything harms your health, whether that be your feelings or thoughts, so always revert to shedding the negative layers you continue to add around you.

Cause and Effect

Model yourself as the creator and as the angels do. They love you without conditions, which means there is nothing any being can say or do to stop that love no matter how horrific. This doesn't mean negative actions are without consequence since each being is creating their own reality every day. They are paying for both positive and poor actions previously made.

What is put out into the Universe is flipped around and multiplied right back to you in this lifetime, the next, and the other worlds and planes beyond. It's the nature of the way that the Universe is laid out. The energy will catch up with you whether you choose to follow the herd as a collective and partake in negative actions, or out of your own independence. The ego drops down into darkness when it has a group to feed off of. It is more likely to contribute negatively to the violent energy being emitted outwardly into the Universe when joining a group to hide behind over hitting the pavement solo.

Every action made has an effect, so in essence the actions you make today are bending the energy around you forming new circumstances that are of equal or greater value to that energy. Regardless if the energy you send out into the ethers is positive or negative, it will multiply. Sometimes what is manifested from that energy can happen almost immediately, while other times it can take anywhere from three to six months on average to transpire.

CHAPTER FOURTEEN

The Balance of Masculine and Feminine Energies

Part of incorporating balance in your life includes balancing the masculine and feminine energies within you. In the next couple of chapters, we'll dive a bit more into what this all means and how it can positively or negatively affect your soul connections with others.

All souls have both masculine and feminine traits and energy within them. When you exude one trait over the other, then you create an imbalance that can lead to complications or challenges. This is similar to giving and receiving gestures, which are both masculine and feminine energy. This doesn't have anything to do with what gender someone identifies themselves to be in this lifetime. When you give you are operating from the masculine energy and when you receive you are operating from the feminine energies.

Masculine energy is external. It is about giving, action, security, and protection. It's putting outward energy into something or someone. It can be promoting yourself and your work. It can be putting effort into a relationship.

Feminine energy is internal. It's about receiving, nurturing and caring. It's being open, compassionate and receptive. It is kindly accepting praise, compliments, or monetary payment for your work. It can be accepting gifts of any type graciously from spirit. It's receiving love with joy from your significant other and showing compassion for them.

When you have trouble with some of the core examples mentioned, then this can indicate the areas where you need to work on increasing your masculine or feminine energies.

Selfish and self-centered behavior isn't masculine or feminine, but one's ego ruling the roost. If there is too much of either a masculine or feminine energy trait in someone, then the scales tip creating an imbalance in your world. An imbalance blocks the flow of positive abundance and blessings to you. It creates other issues such as the selfish and self-centered tendencies example.

Keys to successful relationships sustaining the distance beyond basic attraction, compatibility, and values are balancing these giving and receiving energies. A successful couple is happiest when they exude both masculine and feminine traits. This is regardless of the genders involved in that relationship.

If you have two love partners that are both dominating with too much yang energy or yin energy, then imbalance and issues can arise. It helps when one is more yang (masculine) and one is more yin (feminine) to one extent, but both know to incorporate an efficient amount of masculine and feminine traits. This applies to all couples regardless of their sexual orientation or gender. When looking at power couples that seem to have it down, you'll notice how effortlessly they do this dance of the masculine and feminine energy. It is vacillating back and forth with an equal balance. The more evolved your soul becomes, then the more balanced you become. This balance is balancing both the masculine and feminine energies within you.

American men have the stigma of being previously trained not to show emotional vulnerability. It was insisted by society that they behave in ways that are considered all masculine traits. Their life expectancy ended up being shorter than women since withholding and internalizing emotion can cause health issues later in life. Now it's become more on an equal footing where the life expectancy for both is relatively similar. History has shown this is becoming increasingly less common with the newer and future generations of souls. The younger generations of men display and express more emotion and feeling than the generations of long past. This is creating a more optimum balance within the composites of many men. In fact, some have pointed out there is more emotion in younger men than younger women. Several European countries and other cultures never had the odd stigma of how a man needs to behave and how a woman needs to be based on society's acceptable norms of that time period. They are more soul evolved in that respect.

Everyone has the masculine and feminine traits within them. The traits are perfectly balanced when you are born into an Earthly life. Once society, your peers, and communities get a hold of you with the wretched ego domination, then they can cause future issues within you that can be difficult to reverse through this imbalance of energies. This is through human ego tampering. You've got a required list of rules by society that dictates how you must behave and live your life, which is still going on today in a sense. Except today you just get harshly criticized through social media. They cement it into your psyche on what activities you must partake in. This luckily shifts when your soul leaves the Earth plane and crosses over into the next room. This is when your soul is restored to optimum levels before human tampering entered the equation at that point. This is why it's important to be focused as much as possible now.

Avoid falling into the trap of believing what society and your peers say you must do or how you must act. Refrain from following the herd just because everyone else is doing it. Avoid being influenced by gossip and negativity. Just because a large percentage of people follow and believe that something needs to be a certain way doesn't mean it's true. You are a full-fledged thinking human soul and have an accurate barometer within you on what is right for your soul's journey.

Balancing the Energies in Relationship Connections

When a soul is born into a human body, it has an equal amount of both masculine and feminine traits. A relationship has a brighter chance at success when both partners exude more of one or the other. This has nothing to do with the genders involved. If a girl asks a guy out, then she is the male/masculine energy. When the boy agrees to the date and allows the girl to plan it, then he is the female/feminine energy. It is irrelevant if his overall nature is typically the masculine energy. Masculine/Male energy is the one who initiates, gives, or takes action. The Feminine/Female energy is the one who lets in, receives, or surrenders.

The best scenarios are the couples that have the balance of both energies intertwining. This is by alternating from the masculine to the feminine. Vacillate from being receptive and going along with something (feminine) to the one making the decisions, initiating, and taking action (male).

If the relationship connection is a partnership where you're both the same gender such as two males or two females, then this still applies. One of you needs to be the masculine energy while the other is the feminine energy in order to create a balance within the duo. Human life has trained the masses to see masculine as a man and feminine as a woman, which creates confusion when talking about those energies in spiritual context.

If you have two people exuding masculine energies in any kind of connection, then they might experience some level of discord, arguments, or conflict. If you have two people in a relationship exuding feminine energies in the connection, then nothing gets done and no one asks anyone out or is proactive. There is no movement or anything taking place. You need to have an initiator and a receiver. This also applies to business connections as well as friendships or family member dynamics.

The best of both worlds is where you are alternating between both energies throughout the course and duration of the connection. When one of the partners is always initiating (masculine), then they risk growing frustrated as if they're the one doing all the work. There are cases where one partner initiates and as soon as the other partner finally initiates too, then their mate rejects that initiation. This is because they're both in the masculine role.

When a woman contacts or messages the guy she's interested in to plan to go on a date, then she is now exuding the masculine energy. It may not usually work if the man does not move into the feminine energy as the receiver who accepts her offer at that point. If he's typically used to being the masculine energy, then he will be turned off by a romantic interest being the initiator.

If two people have a romantic interest in one another, and they're both sitting around waiting for the other to make a move by calling, texting, or emailing, then they are both residing in the feminine energy at that moment. What do you think happens in that instance? Nothing. They will wait an eternity for the other to initiate contact. In the end, they may grow frustrated, disheartened, and might temporarily lose interest and move on altogether unless one of them steps into the masculine energy role and takes charge.

Incidentally, I conducted several online polls with single gay men to find out if they preferred to ask a guy out or if they preferred the guy to ask them out. 89% preferred to have the guy ask them out. When you expect someone else to ask you out, then you are operating from the feminine receptive energy. If 89% of the prospects are in the feminine energy, then no one gets asked out. 11% get asked out if there is a match to begin with. The majority of those polled were single and frustrated over having no movement in the love and dating department for a lengthy period of time. They are all waiting for each other to ask the other one out, but there is no one stepping into the initiating masculine energy. There's going to be quite a long wait until that happens. This would also apply to gay women as well too.

The best-case scenario is where the feminine energy person merges into the masculine energy by biting the bullet and going after the one they have their eye on. The other person is still in the feminine receptive energy and therefore accepts the proposal. Now the connection has been made. Movement continues to happen and grow pending they both vacillate between one another's energies accordingly from masculine to feminine.

One woman is the primary breadwinner and makes the bulk of the survival income. She is an executive that runs her own company. Her husband works from home, but doesn't make as much money and takes care of the children. The wife in this scenario is the masculine energy, while her husband is the caring compassionate feminine energy. This doesn't make him any less of a man or her any less of a woman. This relationship works because they have incorporated the right balance of energies.

If a couple is two people of the same gender, then this balance law still applies. If you examine successful long-term unions, then it is likely that you will be able to notice that one of the partners tends to exude the masculine energy while the other is the more feminine energy. They might flip flop where it toggles from masculine energy to the feminine energy field. This is depending on what's going on or what needs to get done. Exceptions can always be made to a generalization.

There is the stereotype that women are looking for emotional support while men are looking for sex. A woman might have a difficult time connecting with a man if she hasn't connected with him on an emotional level. A man might have a difficult time connecting with a woman if he hasn't expressed himself through sex.

This concept applies to the masculine/feminine

energies. If a man or woman is exuding the feminine energy, then he/she will want to connect on an emotional level first. However, a man or woman is exuding masculine energy if he wants to connect on a mental level first. If he feels the person is a buddy type, then he's more open to sex or a relationship with that person.

Same sex couples offer another challenge. Two people of the same gender may seem to be a super easy connection due to both genders understanding what it's like to be that gender, but that's a myth since all people are complicated regardless of their gender or orientation. You could have one male being the more emotional one craving (feminine) emotional support from his partner, while the other (masculine) is less talk and more action. The latter guy is the more masculine energy of the two partners. Two women would be the same concept.

One heterosexual man attempted to debunk the myth that men do not expose their feelings. He is a heterosexual man who said that some have called him sensitive while others have said passionate. He added that he's the type of guy who will fly his fist into a wall, but on the flip side he can write a poem. He wondered if he was too sensitive.

Some women/men want a guy that is sensitive and passionate, rather than distant, aloof, and insensitive.

Sensitivity and being passionate can go hand in hand, but are quite different. Being sensitive can mean that you have an artistic creative side and are in tune to others feelings as well as your own. Passionate is taking that sensitivity to another height. It's sensitivity with some fiery emotions or temperament. It can be someone who is hypersexual and prefers the long sensual kind of lovemaking. It can also be someone that puts their whole selves into whatever they undertake whether it's a career or a relationship. The sensitive more passionate partner is exuding the feminine energy in this state.

If a man in the relationship doesn't feel the support from his partner, whether the partner is a woman or a man, then he will shut down and distance himself. He needs to know his partner is fitting the definition of a "partner". This means the potential mate is much like a business partner where both work together as one having a sense of camaraderie. You offer mutual support the way you would with a best friend.

Relationships reach a place of strain when both partners don't understand when to willingly and graciously give the other partner space as required. Many men primarily need constant bouts of space otherwise the connection will suffocate and so will he. This is why you sometimes hear stories about the guy going out with his buds to have a beer, watch a game, or tinker around with gadgets in the garage. The man in this instance is exuding the masculine energy of strong silence and not needing any kind of emotional distraction, but seeking out an outlet for action. The woman or feminine energy desires to talk about a situation, therefore this person is exuding the feminine energy. This person ends up calling up a friend to gab about it. This energy vacillator applies to all connections regardless if it is romantic, friendship, family, or business, and whether or not it's coming from the man or the woman.

The genders of human souls have drastically shifted to be equal across the board, which means it's now more common to see some women also desiring this space and not wanting to talk about anything serious, while the man wants to talk about it. This is the role reversal of energies we've noticed evolving. Women tend to want to bond even closer to their partner when they're having troubles. The differences of the genders involved are especially evident here. The feminine energy wants to talk about it, while the masculine energy wants to take action to fix it and move on. You also have astrological factors and one's upbringing to consider when studying the complexity of an individual.

With same sex couples there is another rough dynamic depending on what kind of energy the partners exude. I've consulted with same sex couples where there were two males and one of them was the more emotional one demanding constant attention from the other. The more he did that the more the other guy withdrew and grew more distant and less talkative. Pressuring the non-communicative guy to talk will only shut the communication down. A non-talkative guy doesn't open up to emotional demands regardless of his sexual orientation. You likely wouldn't charge at a friend that way, so you'll want to consider approaching the guy as you would one of your friends.

I've also received cases where it's a male-female dynamic with the female wanting to talk to her guy about something, but the more she does, the more the guy pulls further away. The one pulling away is the masculine energy that requires space. The more you hound that person, then the worse it will be. This is because the male/masculine energy prefers to take action to correct something rather than talk about it. It's the same concept as someone who doesn't care for repetitive work-based meetings. They find it to be a waste of time and a bunch of nonsensical hot air blowing around instead of getting to work and doing the job.

During my past work endeavors I was never a fan of the meeting. I found them mostly to be mundane and counterproductive in general. I exude the masculine energy in this case where I prefer diving right on in and doing the work immediately. There are exceptions where sitting down to have a meeting about something is necessary, otherwise give me the bullet points quickly and let's move on and not dwell on it. This is more along the lines of daily meetings as opposed to beneficial once in a while meetings.

There are also male-female dynamic relationships where the female is the one in the masculine role and needing that space, while her man is in the feminine role demanding emotional attention. I've had married men reach out to me to talk about how their wife is dismissive about his feelings, which further points to the energies and how times have changed. Usually it was the wife feeling like the husband was dismissive. This doesn't make anyone less of a man or a woman. This has to do with energies and ensuring that it's balanced within the relationship.

Is there also balance with your work and personal life? One reader named Missy explained that her boyfriend Tom is distant and cold. Tom has compassion and cares, but he doesn't express it the way Missy would like. There is no reassurance about their connection coming from Tom. Missy heads to work where her colleagues are distant and cold as well too. This isn't in a nasty mean way. Her colleague's personalities happen to be the quiet serious distant types that do their job and leave. There is no balance within the team where another personality in the mix offers warm and cheery sociability.

When Missy leaves and goes on a date with Tom, she finds Tom has the same energy as her colleagues. There is no cheer in Missy's life as she prefers a little enthusiasm and personality at some point in her day. This can cause one to feel glum, even if everything in your life is going well. Missy has a job that pays her bills. She has a boyfriend to go on a date with, but she still feels despondent about it. There isn't enough balance of cheer from either her colleagues or the guy she's dating.

Missy used to work the late afternoon shift at work. The team at the company that also worked the afternoon shift were always cheery and sociable brightening up her day. She explained she now works the morning shift where her teammates are quiet and keep to themselves. She said that all would be well if either her current morning shift teammates were bright and cheery, or if her boyfriend was. This is playing a part in the lack of balance in her life. When you're experiencing unhappiness where the source is not understood, then look at the masculine and feminine energies around you and adjust where necessary.

CHAPTER FIFTEEN

Twin Souls
Yin and Yang

God's bright uplifting blinding Light fills the planet, the Universe, all the Galaxies, planes, dimensions from here and beyond. The one area the Light rarely touches are the spaces and pockets of Darkness. It's not that He avoids it like the plague, but there is no love in that space. It's not a pleasant space to reside in for anyone. The exceptions are when a soul cries out for help, then does this Light begin to penetrate the Darkness.

There are two different types of Darkness. There is the Darkness that exists on the Earth plane in a human body within the human ego. There are also the Darkness in the Spirit planes. It is what some have used various names for like Hell, Purgatory, or Limbo. Regardless of the label used to describe it, it's not a place one should desire or thrive to live in. The pain associated with it is unbearable for a soul. There are entities governed by this Darkness that puncture into the Earth plane to enslave as many human beings as possible. You know this has happened when you see a human go corrupt in some way. This is through the avenues of negativity, violence, or hatred of any kind. It is the Darkness that enflames the ego into Darkness.

There is a Light at the end of that Dark tunnel. This is where He exists ready for all that call on Him. Like a stern but loving parent He is always there. He created every space available in all dimensions from here and beyond. He created every living soul and breathed magnificent life into every one of them. He created every soul and every species. Within every soul that incarnates into a human body, He created each soul with the intention of breathing glorious life into them. It may appear to be a complicated design to create a Universe with one planet filled with billions of living souls. This planet whirls around in a vast space filled with billions of miles of other planets and stars soaring for all infinity with no other visible soul or life form except on Earth. This doesn't mean this is the only life form that exists in the billions of infinite miles that go on for an eternity. None of this is an accident and nor is the soul in a human body an accident. The soul came from somewhere important as much as some would like to believe the theory that human beings evolved through the evolution of animals. The animals came from somewhere as did the infinite miles of black space. The consciousness within the soul is the part of you that develops reasoning discernment and skill. It has the capacity to psychically see beyond the surface and what you see or don't see or comprehend with your physical sight.

The soul chooses to incarnate into a human body for an Earthly life for various reasons and purposes. This includes you choosing the two souls that will be your human parents. This is regardless if the child is given up for adoption, raised by a single parent or guardian, or two people of the same gender. It doesn't matter who will raise them, but who they will be born from and why. This is knowing the consequences and risks that will come along with that.

During some human pregnancies, there will be times when an egg is split producing two offspring. These are Earth born siblings called twins. Human twin siblings tend to be exactly identical, nearly identical, or nowhere near identical. They may be identical in looks and/or personality, even though they were split from the same egg, but some human twins also look nothing alike, but may display comparable personality traits. This is similar to the concept of how twin soul flames are born. Human born twins can be twin flames, but this is a rare occurrence unless they tend to share a high measure of spiritual instincts with a deep running psychic line between each other. This same deep running psychic line runs between twin flames. It is one of the reasons they are in tune to each other when they first lock eyes.

The most accurate label is twin souls, but many in the spiritual community are accustomed to calling them twin flames, so we'll continue alternating the label for the sake of comprehending. Twin flames have a shared ongoing sentiment and quest from the moment they're a spark shooting out of God's love that explodes into a blinding white fire that breaks apart causing one to be two until two become one again, separate and whole, and back around again. Each flame understands what God meant when He said, "I am You."

This is because looking into the eyes of your twin flame is like looking into the eyes of God. You can actually see God behind one another's eyes. Suddenly human life makes sense if it didn't before. All souls were born out of His love and will fall right back into that love before being re-born again into that love.

All souls spark out of the same source of energy. This energy source is what some call God, the Light, Energy, the Source, All Knowing, the Creator, the Force, and so on. Differing groups, religions, sects on Earth that choose to follow their own belief system will call it one thing while another will call it something else. It doesn't matter what name a human being chooses to call it and nor does Heaven care what someone calls it, because all that is understood is what is.

When a soul is conceived from this source, it splits into two souls in the same fashion that human twins split off from the same egg. Twin flames are one soul split into two souls from the same source of energy at the same time. All souls are made as one, but then split into pairs for the purpose of having a partner that each soul calls home. Sometimes they connect on Earth and other times they separate to have distinct soul missions.

Yin Yang and Masculine Feminine Energy

Like human twins, twin flame souls also share the traits of being exactly identical, nearly identical, or not identical at all. One half of the twin soul may exude more yang/masculine energy, while the other twin soul half displays more yin/feminine energy. They both vacillate equally between the pair. It doesn't matter what their human gender is as we're talking about energy, which has no physical anatomy.

Within these split aparts, both souls conceived have an equal amount of yang/masculine and yin/feminine energy. This means that all human souls are born with a balance of both male and female energies within them. The goal is to keep that balance present throughout the duration of your Earthly life. This makes for a well-rounded put together human soul operating from the highest consciousness level possible they can achieve under the circumstances.

There are human developed traits that will

prompt someone to display more of one gender energy over another. For example, human men tend to have more testosterone, which causes them to display more male dominated energy, while human women tend to have more estrogen, which prompts them to display more female receptive energy. This varies and moves up and down as the person ages, and depending on that particular person's make-up.

Typically, this energy reverses as one moves into the human thirties and beyond. Men see a significant drop in testosterone with a rise in estrogen, while women see a drop-in estrogen and a rise in testosterone. Part of this change can also be due to environmental factors as well as diet. This definition is separate from what the male and female energy is within the compartments of one God created soul.

There are also men who may exude more feminine energy, while some women may exude more masculine energy. This doesn't make that person any less of a man or a woman. Those myths are due to human ego being taught one thing growing up only to discover there is more going on in the world than they imagined or understood there to be. The energy in the human man or human woman is the gender energy they mostly convey, which has nothing to do with the anatomy you were born with.

Someone in the creative arts will tend to display more feminine energy because creativity is in the realms of that jurisdiction, while someone in construction, building, or the areas of physical sports and activity will display more action masculine oriented energy, regardless if the person was born this lifetime as a man or a woman.

There are also people who may exude a steadiness of both energies, which is the ultimate goal for each soul in order to achieve spiritual balance. This might be where they dive into the creative internal expression world on one day, but the next day they're playing in a sports league to express themselves through action.

Running your own business would fall into the realms of masculine energy, because you're taking action. Taking action is the masculine energy, while thinking creatively outside of the box would fall into the feminine energy side. The best of both worlds is when you are vacillating back and forth between displaying all facets and possibilities that your soul is capable of. This is what the twin flames convey while in one another's presence. When you reach that balanced energy state in life, then it becomes more likely that you would cross paths with your twin flame. Some souls may come exceptionally close to revealing this balance, but then once they bond with the twin flame does that rise to a fuller balance in both parties. This doesn't mean that every single soul that attains that balance will connect with their twin flame, since most twin souls are back home where you are with them indefinitely. There would be little reason for them to incarnate at the same time.

"You complete me" is a famous romantic cliché line that has a measure of truth with all soul mate connections, but even more so with the twin flames.

All souls are expected to find a happy medium where they display an equal amount of balanced masculine energy with feminine energy. Masculine energy is associated with words such as action, giving, aggression, control, and domination. Feminine energy is about traits like receiving, caring, compassion, creativity, and passive aggression. When all human souls show an equal amount of both energies and know when or when not to display one over the other, then you have reached the center and space of where your soul is the most content in its consciousness. It is when your soul is as whole as possible as it was when it was born into an Earthly life.

An interesting example of who displays this balance of twin flame masculine and feminine energy regardless of energy, would be those fictional female outlaw characters in the film, *Thelma and Louise (Susan Sarandon and Geena Davis)* In the film it became Thelma and Louise against the world mirroring one another's personalities like twin souls do, then swapping identities where one is the more masculine energy and the other is the more feminine, only to re-calibrate and re-balance that out by switching and exchanging personality roles in an effortless fluid transaction. The Thelma character becomes the more masculine energy when Louise has fallen into the feminine energy of emotion that causes her to give up hope in that hotel room after discovering their hard-earned money has been stolen by the cowboy drifter *(Brad Pitt)*.

Thelma and Louise were inseparable best friends lacking in the deep kind of romantic love they had with their boyfriend or husband. It was with each other that they had that kind of love that transcends beyond the physical attraction you have between yourself and the mate of your choice. Thelma and Louise become liberated and experience a soulful kind of freedom neither had felt before. Coming together in the way they did coaxed their true natures to take flight just by being in one another's presence in an unforeseen dramatic circumstance.

This has nothing to do with the fictional crimes committed in the film or the fact that they were fleeing from the law. This went deeper and beyond that part of the story, but the underlying focus was rather the spiritual essence moving between their souls that propelled them to keep going and soar off that cliff in the end of heightened transformation that only a twin flame union could produce.

It's helpful to describe the energies by using two people of the same gender. Using the general accepted point of view with the image of a human man and a human woman coming together causes confusion leading one to believe this is the vision of a twin flame. To see the twin soul, one must look beneath the human anatomy and gender to note the soul's overall energy force.

CHAPTER SIXTEEN

Blissful Happy Place

U se an equal balance of logic and emotion. This isn't to be confused with being closed off emotionally with others. This is about avoiding the long fall into the abysmal whirlwind of wasted emotions over something trivial such as a news story, unless you're able to practically do something positive about it. The complaints and constant attacking of others that so many partake in today do nothing to help anyone, except contribute to the noise.

There will continue to be a greater divide, opposing viewpoints, arguments, conflict, and challenges brought on by the darkness of ego. Earthly life will continue to be more of a repeat for those stuck in that rigid mindset. None of that will help to bridge opposing viewpoints until those who are guilty of it learn about the true meaning of having compassion and displaying respect for others. This also means showing those virtues to those you disagree with. It's looking for ways to meet an opponent in the middle.

Avoid obsessing over a media headline as that lowers your vibration, which creates a block. There is nothing positive gained by becoming emotionally invested in a news story. That is the overall theme of modern-day life today in the post technological age. It's time to move the held back consciousness away from that.

There are those who spend each year wishing the previous year would go away. Reality is what you make it, so if you choose to see a year as being miserable, then that's the energy you'll continue to bring in. Moving forward is not going to change anything until you decide to change.

What is one of the steps in Alcoholics Anonymous? God, grant me the serenity to accept the things I cannot change. The courage to change the things I can and the wisdom to know the difference.

Have the perception of a great actor, which is to walk in another's shoes as if you are part of their consciousness. All of this can help in raising your vibration, which will give you stronger psychic input.

Thinking and speaking positive words is preached in nearly most every spiritual or religious circle or group. Overall this wisdom might sound cliché and vaguely generic, but there is a reason this tip is so popular. There is some basis of proven truth to it. Understand the depth of the meaning of thinking, speaking, and feeling positive words. This is telling you that the majority of the time your thoughts and feelings should be on the positive side if you are intending to make a desire come true. You are thinking positive thoughts and speaking positive words whenever you can.

This isn't telling anybody that it's a crime or a sin to fall into negativity on occasion because you will. You are a human being having a human experience that entails all of the colorful ranges of emotions and thoughts based on your current experience.

General spiritual practitioners preach that you be all love and light. If every person on the planet exuded that state, then there would no doubt be peace on Earth. Since this is not a realistic or practical request that the billions of people on the planet are capable of following, we have to examine this on a deeper realistic level. Some recipients have found they've fallen into the cracks of negativity when attempting to move into a permanent love and light state. There are people born with a naturally genuine bubbly personality, but not everyone wakes up in laughing joyful upbeat hysterics ready to seize each day in this manner. In fact, some people might even become a bit skeptical of a personality that exudes that infectious joyful state all day long, while others might say I'll have what that person is having.

Earth would be a blissful awesome place to reside on if every human being on the planet were able to achieve that bright, joyful, goofy, loving life state all day long. Imagine yourself walking around in that state feeling that energy essence throughout each day. It can make you feel good, and bring in more of those good vibrations to you, but that is also not a realistic practical demand to place on a human being.

Every person on the planet is having a specific human experience with trials, tribulations, and challenges, coupled with varying measures of success, good times, and blessings. Everyone would love to have the latter kind of life and state of mind and being where you are filled to the brim of good feelings. Why wouldn't you? Who wants to feel a heavy weight of ugliness sitting on top of you day in and day out? It's an exhausting way to live with such a heavy burden sitting on top of your back.

Find the healthiest balance you can between making changes in your life through baby action steps that will help you achieve a more positive state. At the same time be realistic that you will have setbacks and challenges thrown at you out of nowhere that can throw your life off balance. That equation is inevitable and a part of life. Those types of rougher challenges help you grow, evolve and change.

It's also not a realistic demand to place on the masses to be joyful every second, especially for the millions of people around the world battling mental and emotional health issues and disorders. This is something that touches me on a more personal level. Some were born with that in their disposition, while others developed it over time due to traumatic life experiences. As someone who is included in that statistic of battling mental and emotional health issues, I understand how difficult it can be to keep yourself in balance. Who more appropriate to discuss this with you than someone that understands the nature of the beast by battling with that in daily life.

Bouncing around blissfully all day long is a wonderful space to reside and view circumstances in, but that's not what helps you grow and evolve. It is the hard times and the tough experiences that shape you. That is what assists in the soul's evolving process. This can be seen in the many success stories out there. When you investigate that person's past, you discover they came from some measure of abuse or trials and tribulations that seem more severe than others. They tend to appear composed, centered, and strong with a warrior like stance.

It's inhuman and impractical to be positive and optimistic 100% of the time. Your thoughts and feelings fluctuate throughout each day depending on your mental, emotional, and physical state. The more positive you are, then the better the results. You can get by as long as the ratio of positive is larger than the negative. For example, it can be 75% positive and 25% negative, then the chances of you making a stronger matched vibrational connection with the positive flow of abundance is greater than if those numbers were reversed. If the percentage of negativity you give off is greater than the positive, then it is the negative that will expand and bring more of that to you.

If you're generally a positive person with the occasional negativity that's on the bare minimum side, then the positive quotient is strong enough to make some traction. If you're always negative or you are more negative than positive, then you'll need to work on that. The negative essence is too great and overbearing to bring in something positive. The consequences are that more negativity comes into your life. The more positivity you can conjure up, then the more likely you will be in a state of positive abundance reception.

I've witnessed those who are perpetually negative where they always seem to have one thing going wrong after another in their life. I've also observed those who are typically positive people, and they always seem to have great things going on for them. It's too consistent not to notice this pattern. Many others have noticed this design too, especially abundance preachers, which is why it's one of the hotter tips always made in abundance circles. And that is to be positive!

Being optimistic includes looking for that silver lining when in a crisis. Not only does that help with the abundance attracting business process, but it also helps in re-training your mind to finding creative solutions to issues that arise in your life, rather than seeing the constant bleak hopelessness of where you are currently at today.

It's understood that a major crisis is expected to create upset. It also depends on what one views a crisis to be. In the latter years, any crises and drama that has taken place around me throughout the course of my life was taken in stride. When I was younger and immature, my reaction was more aggressive and erratic. That's one of the things you hope tempers with age or during your soul's evolvement progress. A legitimate major crisis would be losing a loved one, but a false major crisis might be one's obsession over a gossip media story that pushes you to see it as the end of the world. It's generally not the end of the world and you move onto the next gossip media story.

Many around me have commented that I seem to be the calm inside the storm or that my emotional reaction to things is on an even keel, while others might have a harder time with managing dramatic curve balls thrown at them. Their stress, anger, and upset will shoot from 0-100 in the span of five seconds. Others will skyrocket past that as you may likely recall seeing them in hysterics making all kinds of noise.

You might also be aware and conscious enough to notice some that rise in anger and upset tantrum energy. They are catapulted into the sphere of creating a domino effect of negative circumstances into their life preceding that. When you then look at those that reveal a calmer demeanor while in crises, you may note how strong and in control they are over an issue. Circumstances tend to go much smoother for those personality types. They also make exceptional leaders who can take care of emergencies as swiftly as a Fireman answering a bell. Obviously, the latter tend to be people that are destined trailblazers.

A great leader has calm strong composure most of the time like my 15th second cousin Queen

Elizabeth I, who also shared my life path number 1 for those numerology lovers. When the life path number 1 is showcasing the best parts of themselves, they are ordained to lead in some way. The negatives are the opposite of that which can be domination, but don't worry I'm pretty regal and composed like Elizabeth.

Human beings were designed to be a fully-fledged thinking feeling consciousness. We get moody, stressed, upset, depressed and on and on. This isn't about denying those feelings and thoughts when you move into that space. Feel your feelings, think your thoughts, and be aware and mindful of them. Don't feel guilty about experiencing rough feelings. This is about having the additional awareness of everything that is happening around you. This helps in being completely conscious of when you've hit a negative state. Look at what can be done about it. Examine what caused it and what you can do to remedy it.

Don't fake positivity if you're not feeling that. Avoid kicking or beating yourself up if you find it impossible to pretend to be happy if that's not your current disposition. It takes time to work on becoming more of an optimistic positive person. Cut yourself some slack and focus on working on being more aware of your overall thoughts and feelings. If it's always negative, then work on attempting to shift that into something positive at least once a day if even for a few minutes at a time. The more you put that into practice, the easier it gets before you find it happens effortlessly and naturally.

When you're asked to be positive and optimistic, this also means that you need to be more positive than negative. This is cutting you some slack and giving you a bit of leeway to be negative on occasion. This doesn't mean be negative deliberately because you're allowed.

This would apply to those who are told, "You're too negative."

They're response is, "I don't care, I'm mad and they all need to know."

Do they really need to know or is your ego bruised about something? The Devil works in mysterious ways as God does. The Darkness ensures you remain stuck in a negative state. The Darkness part of the Devil is not to be confused with the Dark that some light spirits reside in because they understand it well. Statistics have revealed that a higher number of people believe in the possibility of God, but a far lower number believe in the possibility of the Devil. How can one witness the dark demonic behavior of humankind day after day and not suspect that there is a something more sinister interfering? The sinister energy comes from within the darkness of ego that resides in each human soul.

When you fall into negativity, then recognize when you have. Work on improving that state again without guilt of having fallen into a downtrodden state, since guilt can lower your vibration. Your overall demeanor is content and at peace, with the occasional hiccups that come in here and there. Involve prayer, meditation, and quiet retreats into your life. You can do this anywhere that helps you move into a more serene state, such as at home in a private space or go to a quiet nature locale.

You can get to an optimistic space easier if you take a step back to acknowledge the positive things you're grateful for in your life today. You can move closer in that direction if you focus on hobbies and activities that make you smile, rather than doing things that aggravate your natural centered state of being.

Acknowledge the blessings you have today that may sometimes be taken for granted until it's taken away. Are you able to live in the place you currently live in comfortably knowing your bills are getting paid? Then that's something to be grateful for. You're not on the streets with nowhere to go and no one to turn to. Do you have a car or a mode of transportation to get you to work and other places you need to go to? That's another blessing.

Make a list of the things you're grateful for in your life today. Type it out in an email to yourself. The benefit of that is it helps you to take a few minutes to think about the things that are working in your life. If it's something that seems insignificant, write it down anyway. As you're writing it out, you're taking that moment to acknowledge its existence through focus while marinating in that thought and feeling of gratitude. You start to feel a bit better in the process. You might even have that moment of clarity that you do indeed have some things that are working.

It's human nature to constantly seek out and obtain things. You obtain one thing, then you're quickly onto the next. This is followed by disregarding what you just achieved instead of taking that extra moment to realize how grateful and blessed you are in that moment for obtaining what you originally sought out.

I thank God and my Spirit team daily for the blessings that come into my life. If I need assistance with something or someone, I will request it in prayer. Once it pans out well, then I quickly thank my Spirit team. I've said things like, "I don't want you to think I don't acknowledge what just took place. I am highly aware of how you've just helped me with this, and I thank you. Thank you for putting up with me and for helping me with this."

Because I know what a pain I can be at times, even though from spirits perspective they are unfazed about that.

You can have whatever it is you desire, pending it is aligned with your higher self. You are a master magician able to create all of the wonders you've always longed for right there in your mind. This is the first place that the manifestation process begins. What an amazing power you have to be able to access all of that right within you. You don't need any divination tools, nor do you need to recite any special invocations, unless that's something you enjoy doing, but in the end it's not necessary. Move the thoughts in your mind right into your soul's spirit. Use those psychic clair sense channels you have built into you since the birth of your soul that allows you to have a direct communication line with Heaven any time, day, or place. God gave this to you so that you can access Him whenever you like. It's like a good parent that gives you a phone line to them whenever you want or need it.

Feeling positive and optimistic means not only are you thinking and speaking positivity and radiating optimism, but you are also feeling positive and optimistic. You feel this energy essence all throughout your body, mind, and soul. Feel and experience God's white light energy throughout your body now. This means allowing yourself to feel it within and around you and your aura. This uplifting positive white light energy is rising from the Earth's ground, through your entire being and spreading throughout all your senses. It expands to ten feet, then twenty and thirty feet around you. You feel this on a massive level as it blasts out of you and upwards making a solid connection with God and with Heaven.

Imagine this light clearing away anything considered negative or toxic. This abundant uplifting optimism moves through your physical body. It penetrates your mind awakening it. Your perception grows to become more transcendent and deeper than you've ever experienced. Your spirit and soul are blasted with white light raising your vibration into the Heavens, which balances all aspects of your mind, body, and soul. You have now moved into the realms of becoming a powerful positive manifester!

Acknowledgments

Thank you to God, my Spirit Team Council, and to all of the loyal readers that have hopped on this awesome train ride of mine and stayed on. I am forever blessed and grateful for your eternal support of the work we do. Thank you also for supporting the arts and the artists of the world.

ALSO BY KEVIN HUNTER

Stay Centered Psychic Warrior
Warrior of Light
Empowering Spirit Wisdom
Darkness of Ego
Realm of the Wise One
Transcending Utopia
Reaching for the Warrior Within
Spirit Guides and Angels
Soul Mates and Twin Flames
Raising Your Vibration
Divine Messages for Humanity
Connecting with the Archangels
Monsters and Angels
The Seven Deadly Sins
Love Party of One
Twin Flame Soul Connections
A Beginner's Guide to the Four Psychic Clair Senses
Tarot Card Meanings
Attracting in Abundance
Abundance Enlightenment
Living for the Weekend
Ignite Your Inner Life Force
Awaken Your Creative Spirit
The Essential Kevin Hunter Collection
Metaphysical Divine Wisdom (Series)

STAY CENTERED PSYCHIC WARRIOR
A Psychic Medium's Trip Through the Darkness and Light of the Spirit Worlds, and Other Paranormal Phenomena

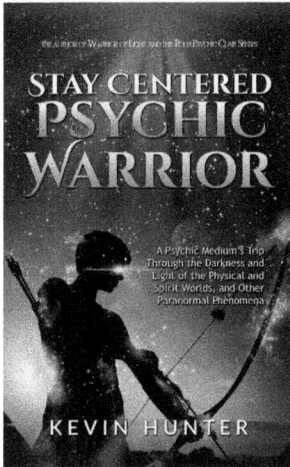

In *Stay Centered Psychic Warrior*, metaphysical teacher, psychic, medium, and author, Kevin Hunter talks about what it's like battling between mental health issues and the deeply potent psychic input that continuously falls into his soul's consciousness throughout each day. He offers plenty of examples and discussions of his brushes with spirit, seeing and hearing the dead, the power of the Darkness and the Light in both the physical and spirit worlds, along with sharing his numerous personal psychic and mediumship essays, glimpses of the Other Side, near death experiences, past lives, soul contracts, traveling to and from the Spirit Worlds, spirit guides and angels, recognizing your own psychic gifts, and much more!

This unique autobiography focuses on psychic and mediumship related content coupled with the soul's journey and purpose. Stay Centered Psychic Warrior is an intensely forceful and revealing read that doesn't shy away from the uncomfortable, the Darkness, abuse, mental health issues, while uplifting it with the many blessings of the Light and intriguing day to day psychic phenomena all in one. Allow it to inspire you to recognize your own psychic gifts knowing there is much more to this Earthly life than can be seen or comprehended. Be empowered to break through the rubble and stand strong and centered under the powerful Light that shines through any Darkness.

A Beginner's Guide to the
FOUR PSYCHIC CLAIR SENSES

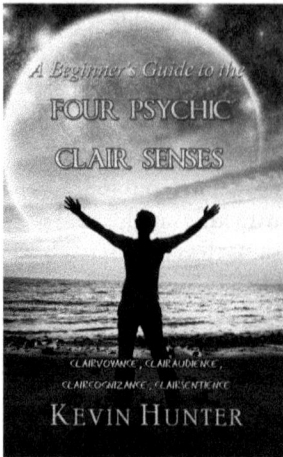

Many believe psychic gifts are bestowed upon select chosen ones, while others don't believe in the craft at all. The reality is every soul is born with heightened psychic gifts and capabilities, but somewhere along the way those senses have dimmed. All are capable of being a conduit with the other side, including those closed off and blocked to it. There are a variety of enlightened beings residing in the spirit realms to assist human souls that request their help. They use varying means and methods to communicate with you called clair channels. These clairs are crystal clear etheric senses used to communicate with any higher being, spirit guide, angel, departed loved one, archangel, and God.

The *Four Psychic Clair Senses* illustrates what the core senses are, examples of how the author picks up on messages, how you can recognize the guidance, and other fun metaphysical psychic stuff. You are a walking divination tool that allows you to communicate with Spirit. The clairs enable you to receive heavenly messages, guidance, and information that positively assist you or another along your Earthly journey. Read about the four core clairs in order to pinpoint what best describes you and how to have a better understanding of what they are and how they work for you.

TAROT CARD MEANINGS

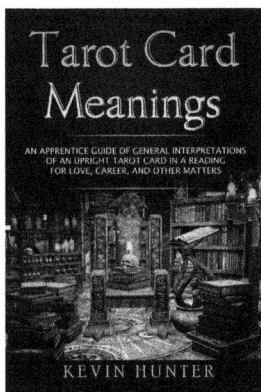

Tarot Card Meanings is an encyclopedia reference guide that takes the Tarot apprentice reader through each of the 78 Tarot Cards offering the potential general meanings and interpretations that could be applied when conducting a reading. The meanings included can be applied to most anything whether it be spiritual, love, general, or work-related questions.

Many novices struggle with reading the Tarot as they want to know what a card can mean in their readings. They grow stuck staring at three cards side by side and having no idea what it could be telling them. The Tarot Card Meanings book can assist by pointing you in the general direction of where to look. It will not give you the ultimate answers and should not be taken verbatim, as that is up to you as the reader to come to that conclusion. The more you practice, read, and study the Tarot, then the better you become.

Tarot Card Meanings avoids diving into the Tarot history, or card spreads and symbolism, but instead focuses solely on the potential meaning of a card in a general, love, or work reading. This gives you a structure to jump off of, but it is up to you to take that energy and add the additional layers to your reading, while trusting your higher self, intuition, instincts and Spirit team's guidance and messages. Anything included in the Tarot Card Meanings book is an overview and not intended to be gospel. It is merely one suggested version of the potential meanings of each of the 78 Tarot cards in a reading. It may assist the novice that is having trouble interpreting cards for themselves.

ALSO AVAILABLE BY KEVIN HUNTER

Books that Empower, Enlighten, Educate, and Entertain!

*Just as your body needs physical food to survive,
your soul needs spiritual food for well-being nourishment.*

THE ESSENTIAL KEVIN HUNTER COLLECTION

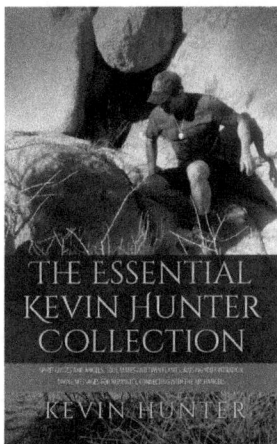

Kevin Hunter an empowering author specializing in a variety of genres, but he is most notably known for his work in the realms of spirituality, metaphysical, and self-help. He has assisted people around the world with standing in their power, and in having a stronger connection with Heaven, while navigating the materialistic practical world. Now some of his popular spiritually based books are available in this one gigantic volume.

The Essential Kevin Hunter Collection is the spiritual bible that contains over 500 pages of content geared towards improving and enhancing your life. It is for those who prefer to have everything in one gigantic book. The content included in this edition are from the books: *Spirit Guides and Angels, Soul Mates and Twin Flames, Raising Your Vibration, Divine Messages for Humanity, Connecting with the Archangels, Warrior of Light, Empowering Spirit Wisdom, and Darkness of Ego.*

THE ESSENTIAL
KEVIN HUNTER
COLLECTION

Featuring the following books:
Warrior of Light, Empowering Spirit Wisdom, Darkness of Ego,
Spirit Guides and Angels, Soul Mates and Twin Flames, Raising
Your Vibration, Divine Messages for Humanity, and Connecting
with the Archangels.

TRANSCENDING UTOPIA
Reopening the Pathway to Divinity

Transcending Utopia is packed with practical and spirit knowledge that focuses on enhancing your life through empowering divinely guided spiritual related teachings, inspiration, wisdom, guidance, and messages. The way to accelerate existence on Earth towards Utopia is if every person on the planet resided in their soul's true nature, which is in a state of all love, joy, and peace. The ultimate Nirvana is surpassing that perfection through methods that a limited consciousness could ever dream possible. This is the exceptional glory your soul was born into before the dense turbulence of Earthly life enveloped and suffocated you.

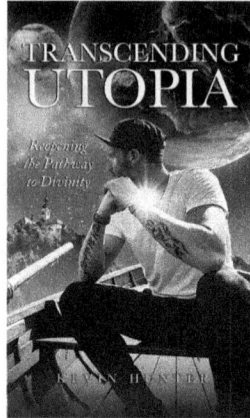

Transcending Utopia is to go beyond your limits and travel outside of the generic mundane materialistic achievement that human beings taught one another to thrive for. A utopian society is where everything is perfectly blissful on all levels according to the sanctified values you were born with. The sensations connected to how flawless everything feels in that moment reveals the authentic perfection you were made from. Utopia is the ideal paradise as imagined in one's dreams that seems to be inaccessible by human standards. It is a state of mind that is possible to reach by adopting broader ways of looking at circumstances while being disciplined about how you conduct your life. You search for a sign of this utopia through external means, only to be consistently left with disappointment. This is because utopia begins and ends inside the spark that burns within your spirit like a pilot light waiting to be ignited.

LIVING FOR THE WEEKEND
The Winding Road Towards Balancing
Career Work and Spiritual Life

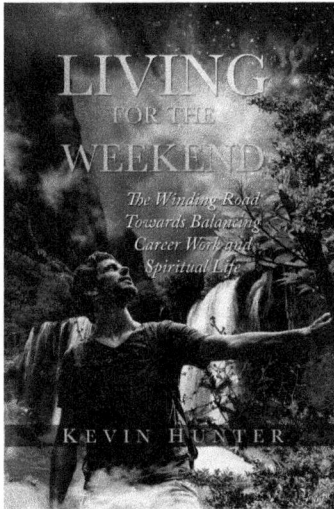

Working hard to ensure your bills are paid can leave your soul spiritually starved for soul nourishment. When your ultimate goal is to obtain enough money to be comfortable that you become carried away in that current, then there is little to no room for Divine enrichment.

Many work to survive in jobs they hate because it's the way it is. As a result, they experience and endure all sorts of emotional pain whether it is through depression, sadness, anger, or any other kind of negative stressor. Some silently suffer through this emotional strain gradually killing off their life force. If you don't have a healthy social life and positive fun filled activities and hobbies to balance that burden outside of that, then that could add additional tension. What's it all for if you can't live the life you've always wanted to live? Instead, you spend your days growing forever miserable and broken.

Living for the Weekend examines the pitfalls, struggles, as well as the benefits available in the current modern-day working world. This is followed up with spiritual and practical tips, guidance, messages, and discussions on ways to incorporate more balance and enlightenment to a cutthroat material driven world.

Attracting in Abundance
Opening the Divine Gates to Inviting in Blessings and Prosperity
Through Body, Mind, and Soul Spirit

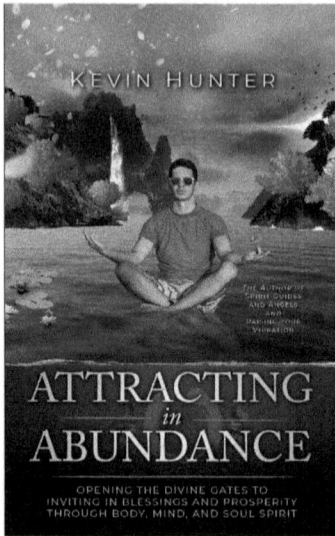

Having enough money to survive comfortably enough on this physical plane is part of obtaining abundance, but it's not the destination and purpose to thrive for. You could work hard to make enough money to the point you are set for life, but that won't necessarily equate to happiness. Achieving a content satisfied state of joy and serenity starts with examining your soul's state and overall well-being. When that's in place, then the rest will follow.

Attracting in Abundance combines practical and spirit wisdom surrounding the nature of abundance. This is something that most everyone can get on board with because all human beings desire physical comforts, blessings, and prosperity, regardless of their personal values and belief systems. *Attracting in Abundance* is broken up into three parts to help move you towards inviting abundance into your life on all levels. "Part One" contains some no-nonsense lectures surrounding the philosophies, concepts, and debates on the laws of attracting in abundance. "Part Two" is the largest of the sections geared towards fine tuning the soul into preparing for abundance. "Part Three" is the final lesson plan to help crack open the gates of abundance with various helpful tidbits, guidance, and messages as well as the blocks that can prevent abundance from coming in.

The B-Side to the Attracting in Abundance book

ABUNDANCE ENLIGHTENMENT
*An Easy Motivational Guide to
the Laws of Attracting in Abundance
and Transforming Your Soul*

Ultimate authentic success surrounds your soul's growth and evolving process. It's when you realize that none of the physical ego driven desires matter in the end. You can work hard to make sure you stay afloat, you're able to pay your bills, and support yourself and family, but you're not chasing popularity for external validation. Any amount of goodness displayed from your heart is the true measure of real accomplishment.

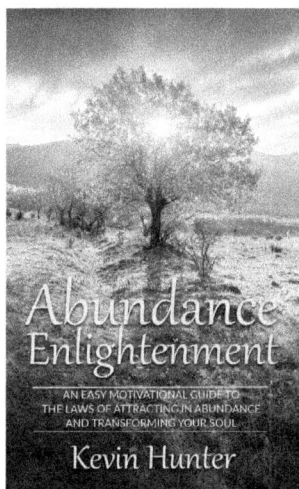

An overflowing feeling of optimism and love coupled with faith and action is what increases the chances of attracting good things and positive experiences to you. Abundance is more than monetary and financial increase. It can also be about reaching an optimistic well-being state of joy, peace, and love. This positive emotional mindful state simultaneously attracts in blessings.

Abundance Enlightenment is the follow up book to *Attracting in Abundance*. It contains both practical guidance and spirit wisdom that can be applied to everyday life. Some of the key topics surround the laws of attraction as well as healthier money management and improving your soul to help make you a fine tuned in abundance attractor.

MONSTERS AND ANGELS
*An Empath's Guide to Finding Peace in a Technologically Driven
World Ripe with Toxic Monsters and Energy Draining Vampires*

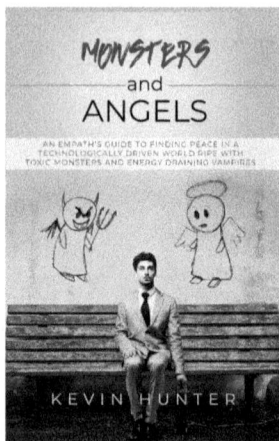

Every person on the planet is capable of being empathic and sensitive, to becoming an energy vampire or toxic monster. No one is exempt from displaying the darker sides of their ego. The easiest and most efficient way to spread any kind of energy is online. Every time you log onto the Internet, there is a larger chance you're going to see something related to the news, media, or gossip areas thrown in front of you, even if you attempt to avoid it as much as possible. You're absorbing everything that your consciousness faces, including the ugly and the wicked, which has its own consequences. This tempestuous energy is tossed into the Universe ultimately creating a flame-throwing battleground inside and around you.

Monsters and Angels discusses how technology, media, and social media have an immense power in distributing both positive and negative influences far and wide. This is about being mindful of what can negatively affect your state of being, and how to counter and avoid that when and wherever possible. This is why it's beneficial to govern yourself, your life, and your surroundings like a strict disciplined executive.

TWIN FLAME SOUL CONNECTIONS
Recognizing the Split Apart, the Truths and Myths of Twin Flames,
Soul Love Connections, Soul Mates, and Karmic Relationships

Twin Flames have a shared ongoing sentiment and quest from the moment they're a spark shooting out of God's love that explodes into a blinding white fire that breaks apart causing one to be two, until two become one again, separate and whole, and back around again. Looking into the eyes of your Twin Flame is like looking into the eyes of God, because to know love is to know God.

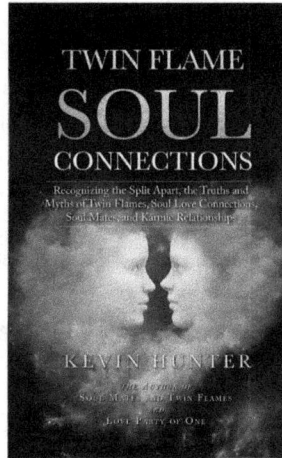

TWIN FLAME
SOUL
CONNECTIONS
Recognizing the Split Apart, the Truths and Myths of Twin Flames, Soul Love Connection, Soul Mates, and Karmic Relationships

KEVIN HUNTER
THE AUTHOR OF
SOUL MATES AND TWIN FLAMES
LOVE PARTY OF ONE

Twin Flame Soul Connections discusses and lists some of the various myths and truths surrounding the Twin Flames, and how to identify if you've come into contact with your Twin Flame, or if you know someone who has. The ultimate goal is not to find ones Twin Flame, but to awaken one's heart to love, and to work on becoming complete and whole as an individual soul through spiritual self-mastery, life lessons, growth, and raising your consciousness. Your soul's life was born out of love and will die right back into that love.

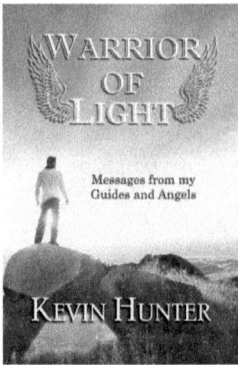

WARRIOR OF LIGHT
Messages from my Guides and Angels

There are legions of angels, spirit guides, and departed loved ones in heaven that watch and guide you on your journey here on Earth. They are around to make your life easier and less stressful. Learn how you can recognize the guidance of your own Spirit team of guides and angels around you. Author, Kevin Hunter, relays heavenly guided messages about getting humanity, the world, and yourself into shape. He delivers the guidance passed onto him by his own Spirit team on how to fine tune your body, soul and raise your vibration. Doing this can help you gain hope and faith in your own life in order to start attracting in more abundance.

EMPOWERING SPIRIT WISDOM
A Warrior of Light's Guide on Love, Career and the Spirit World

Kevin Hunter relays heavenly, guided messages for everyday life concerns with his book, *Empowering Spirit Wisdom*. Some of the topics covered are your soul, spirit and the power of the light, laws of attraction, finding meaningful work, transforming your professional and personal life, navigating through the various stages of dating and love relationships, as well as other practical affirmations and messages from the Archangels. Kevin Hunter passes on the sensible wisdom given to him by his own Spirit team in this inspirational book.

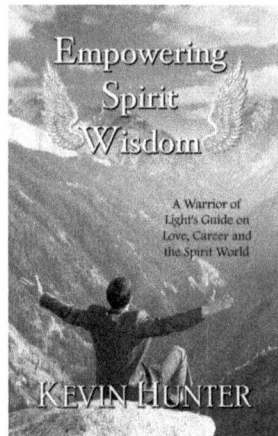

DARKNESS OF EGO

In *Darkness of Ego*, author Kevin Hunter infuses some of the guidance, messages, and wisdom he's received from his Spirit team surrounding all things ego related. The ego is one of the most damaging culprits in human life. Therefore, it is essential to understand the nature of the beast in order to navigate gracefully out of it when it spins out of control. Some of the topics covered in *Darkness of Ego* are humanity's destruction, mass hysteria, karmic debt, and the power of the mind, heaven's gate, the ego's war on love and relationships, and much more.

REACHING FOR THE WARRIOR WITHIN

Reaching for the Warrior Within is the author's personal story recounting a volatile childhood. This led him to a path of addictions, anxiety and overindulgence in alcohol, drugs, cigarettes and destructive relationships. As a survival mechanism, he split into many different "selves". He credits turning his life around, not by therapy, but by simultaneously paying attention to the messages he has been receiving from his Spirit team in Heaven since birth.

REALM OF THE WISE ONE

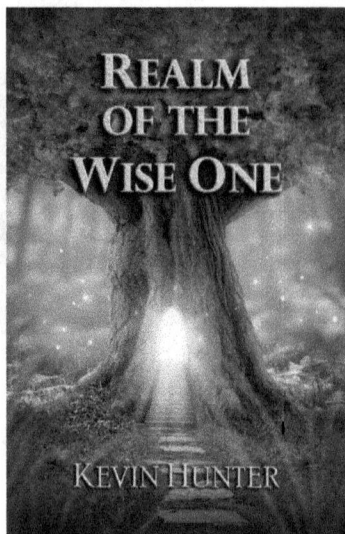

In the Spirit Worlds and the dimensions that exist, reside numerous kingdoms that house a plethora of Spirits that inhabit various forms. One of these tribes is called the Wise Ones, a darker breed in the spirit realm who often chooses to incarnate into a human body one lifetime after another for important purposes.

The *Realm of the Wise One* takes you on a magical journey to the spirit world where the Wise Ones dwell. This is followed with in-depth and detailed information on how to recognize a human soul who has incarnated from the Wise One Realm. Author, Kevin Hunter, is a Wise One who uses the knowledge passed onto him by his Spirit team of Guides and Angels to relay the wisdom surrounding all things Wise One. He discusses the traits, purposes, gifts, roles, and personalities among other things that make up someone who is a Wise One. Wise Ones have come in the guises of teachers, shaman, leaders, hunters, mediums, entertainers and others. *Realm of the Wise One* is an informational guide devoted to the tribe of the Wise Ones, both in human form and on the other side.

IGNITE YOUR INNER LIFE FORCE

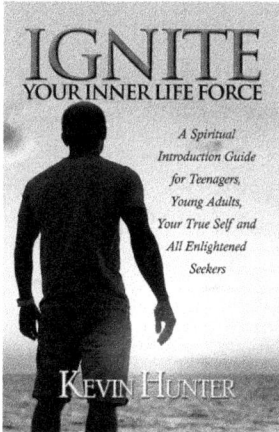

Ignite Your Inner Life Force is an introduction guide for teens, young adults, and anyone seeking answers, messages, and guidance and surrounding spiritual empowerment. This is from understanding what Heaven, the soul, and spiritual beings are to knowing when you are connecting with your Spirit team of Guides and Angels. Some of the topics covered are communicating with Heaven, working with your Spirit team, what your higher self is, your life purpose and soul contract, what the ego is, love and relationships, your vibration energy, shifting your consciousness and thinking for yourself even when you stand alone. This is an in-depth primer manual offering you foundation as you find a higher purpose navigating through your personal journey in today's modern-day practical world.

AWAKEN YOUR CREATIVE SPIRIT

Your creative spirit is more than being artistic and getting involved in creativity pursuits, although this is a good part of it. When your creative spirit is activated by a high vibration state of being, then this is the space you create from. You can apply this to your dealings in life, your creative and artistic pursuits, and to having a greater communication line with your Spirit team on the Other Side. *Awaken Your Creative Spirit* is an overview of what it means to have access to Divine assistance and how that plays a part in arousing the muse within you in order to bring your state of mind into a happier space.

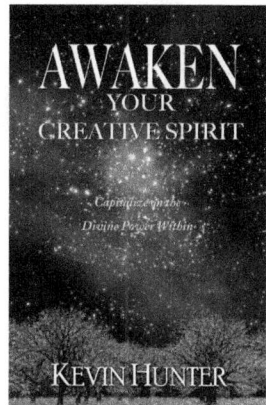

THE *WARRIOR OF LIGHT* SERIES OF POCKET BOOKS

Spirit Guides and Angels, Soul Mates and Twin Flames, Raising Your Vibration, Connecting with the Archangels, Twin Flame Soul Connections, Attracting in Abundance, Monsters and Angels, The Four Psychic Clair Senses, The Seven Deadly Sins, Love Party of One, Abundance Enlightenment, and Divine Messages for Humanity

METAPHYSICAL DIVINE WISDOM
BOOK SERIES

On Psychic Spirit Team Heaven Communication
On Soul Consciousness and Purpose
On Increasing Prayer with Faith for an Abundant Life
On Balancing the Mind, Body, and Soul
On Manifesting Fearless Assertive Confidence
On Universal, Physical, Spiritual and Soul Love

♥

About Kevin Hunter

Kevin Hunter is the metaphysical author of dozens of spiritually based books that include *Warrior of Light, Transcending Utopia, Stay Centered Psychic Warrior, Metaphysical Divine Wisdom Series, Empowering Spirit Wisdom, Realm of the Wise One, Reaching for the Warrior Within, Darkness of Ego, Living for the Weekend, Ignite Your Inner Life Force, Awaken Your Creative Spirit,* and *Tarot Card Meanings.*

His pocketbooks include, *Spirit Guides and Angels, Soul Mates and Twin Flames, Raising Your Vibration, Divine Messages for Humanity, Connecting with the Archangels, The Seven Deadly Sins, Four Psychic Clair Senses, Monsters and Angels, Twin Flame Soul Connections, Attracting in Abundance, Love Party of One* and *Abundance Enlightenment.* His non-spiritual related works include the horror drama, *Paint the Silence,* and the modern-day love story, *Jagger's Revolution.*

Kevin started out in the entertainment business in 1996 as the personal development assistant guy to one of Hollywood's most respected acting talents, Michelle Pfeiffer, at her former boutique production company, Via Rosa Productions. She dissolved her company after several years and he made a move into coordinating film productions for the studios. His film credits include *One Fine Day, A Thousand Acres, The Deep End of the Ocean, Crazy in Alabama, The Perfect Storm, Original Sin, Harry Potter & the Sorcerer's Stone, Dr. Dolittle 2,* and *Carolina.* He considers himself a beach bum born and raised in Southern California. For more information and books visit: www.kevin-hunter.com